Michael Price

Computer Basics

in easy steps

In easy steps is an imprint of In Easy Steps Limited
Southfield Road · Southam
Warwickshire CV47 0FB · United Kingdom
www.ineasysteps.com

7th Edition

Notice of Liability
Every effort has been made to ensure that this book contains accurate
and current information. However, In Easy Steps Limited and the
author shall not be liable for any loss or damage suffered by readers
as a result of any information contained herein.

Trademarks
Microsoft® and Windows® are registered trademarks of Microsoft
Corporation. All other trademarks are acknowledged as belonging to
their respective companies.

Printed and bound in the United Kingdom

ISBN-13 978-1-84078-361-2
ISBN-10 1-84078-361-3

Contents

5 Communication   69

6 Surfing the Internet   91

7 Personal Internet   115

11 Gadgets and Gizmos 191

12 Manage Your Computer 213

Glossary 229

Index 235

1 Choose a Computer

This chapter discusses the differences between computers – Mainframe and PC, laptop and desktop, Apple Mac and Windows, to help you choose your system.

What is a Computer?

Computers are essentially machines which accept sets of instructions (known as programs) and perform computations based on those instructions. The first computers were very large and demanded huge amounts of power. They were used for specialised calculations such as trajectories (astronomical or military), code breaking or weather forecasting.

Hot tip

In this book we will be looking at personal computers suitable for the home and small business, and at the software programs that these use. We'll also take a look at some of the devices that can be attached.

As they developed, computers were made smaller, less power-hungry and less expensive. This led to the introduction of personal computers, intended to support the requirements of individuals and small groups, not just business and government.

Hot tip

This shows three of the early personal computers manufactured by IBM, Apple and Compaq.

Although these machines may look old-fashioned, they included all the essential elements that you'll find in every computer, in one form or another:

- Input   e.g.   keyboard and mouse
- Processing   manipulation and computation
- Output   display and print
- Storage   data and programs
- Operating System   to manage the data and programs
- Communications   links to other computers

These original computers illustrate the two main classes of personal computer – Apple Mac and IBM compatible. They also demonstrate the three main styles:

Desktop Computers

These are mains powered and have several individual components – display, keyboard and system unit (containing the processor, memory and storage elements). Literally desktop to begin with, the system unit is often effectively turned on its side to become a tower unit which is placed beneath the desk.

Hot tip

The distinguishing factor between these is the operating system. IBM-compatibles run Microsoft Windows, while Apple Mac computers run the proprietary Mac OS.

Don't forget

This is a tower format IBM-compatible personal computer, the Dell Precision 390.

Laptop Computers

These are designed to be carried, and contain all of the components (including battery power) in one physical box. Some models emphasize lightness and ultra-portability, others offer the full function of a desktop computer in a space saving format.

All-in-One Computers

These machines are really a hybrid of the desktop and laptop machines, incorporating the components that are usually found in the system unit into the housing for the display unit. This provides a compact and usually very stylish design, but these systems are not particularly portable and they will need access to mains power.

Hot tip

These examples of laptop and all-in-one personal computers are from Apple, and show the Macbook and the iMac. There are also many IBM-compatible laptop and all-in-one computers.

Operating Systems

The operating system on the personal computer is software that manages the computer memory, storage and devices, and provides an interface to access those resources. It processes data and user input, allocating and managing tasks and services for the user and the programs running on the system. It supports communication between computers and networks, and manages the files on the computer disk drives.

There are two predominant operating systems for personal computers, reflecting the two predominant types of personal computer:

Mac OS

This is a graphical operating system developed and marketed by Apple and pre-loaded on Apple Macintosh computers. The current version is Mac OS X which is based on the Unix operating system used by larger scale computers.

Don't forget

The original Mac OS was designed to use the Power PC processor. Mac OS X added support for the Intel Processor (as used by IBM compatible PCs). Mac OS X versions are named after big cats.

V10.0   Cheetah
V10.1   Puma
V10.2   Jaguar
V10.3   Panther
V10.4   Tiger
V10.5   Leopard

10

Hot tip

Applications must be specifically written for the Mac OS. Windows applications won't run, though major applications are available in both operating environments.

There are numerous applications and utilities supplied with Mac OS X. Other applications are available from Apple, Adobe, Microsoft and other suppliers.

Windows

This runs on all IBM-compatible computers which account for over 90% of all personal computers, and it is by far the most commonly used operating system.

The current version is Windows Vista, which is provided in a number of editions designed to suit particular types of user. For home and small office users there are three editions:

- Windows Vista Home Basic
- Windows Vista Home Premium
- Windows Vista Ultimate

Two editions are provided for businesses and large organizations:

- Windows Vista Business
- Windows Vista Enterprise

There is an edition that is designed for beginning users on low powered PCs, in the emerging technology markets:

- Windows Vista Starter

This is shipped on lower-cost computers sold by original equipment manufacturers (OEMs) and Microsoft OEM distributors in 139 countries. However, this edition is not available in the developed technology markets such as the United States, the European Union, Australia, or Japan.

Don't forget

The Ultimate edition of Windows Vista contains all the features from the home and business editions, plus some additional features: the Ultimate Extras.

Beware

There are Home Basic N and Business N editions for Europe that ship without the Windows Media Player.

PC Versus Mac

The best system for you depends on your particular requirements and circumstances, so there's no definitive answer. However these are some of the factors you may wish to take into account while deciding between a Mac and an IBM compatible PC.

Design and Appearance

The PC is usually a fairly bland box of equipment, with some honorable exceptions such as Sony's VAIO laptops.

The Mac is generally considered to be the epitome of elegance and design. There are some issues that might disconcert PC users – the lack of right mouse button on Mac laptops and the keyboard differences. These will be part of the learning curve.

Range of Options

PC system specifications are flexible and low end machines are likely to be cheaper, since there are competing brands, multiple suppliers and a variety of prices and quality levels. There's also a large choice of applications, since the majority of software is programmed for Windows systems.

With the Mac there are limited choices of specification and you are essentially buying everything from the one company.

Specialized Systems

For some users the single manufacturer approach becomes a strength, for example in niche areas such as the media industry. Publishing, film editing, photo editing and audio recording software products were developed first for the Mac (though these suites are now released on PC as well).

Robust Systems

The Mac features an operating system that is claimed to be simpler, more streamlined and more stable than Microsoft Windows. It is also more secure – perhaps because, as a minority product, it just doesn't get targeted as much by the malicious software threats that are endemic to Windows.

Gaming

If your main interest is gaming, a Windows PC is recommended. There's a much larger selection of games, hardware can be optimized for gaming performance, and new titles will always appear first for the Windows machines. There is no native DirectX support in Mac OS (although there are emulators).

Peer Support

If you don't already have experience with computers, you could well allow your choice to be influenced by your family, friends and potential computer teachers and follow their lead.

Office Functions

Both systems can be used for functions such as Internet browsing, document manipulation, scheduling and multimedia playback, and they both support Office functions such as word processing, spreadsheets and presentations. However, if you need to exchange documents with other users, check what they are using, to avoid compatibility problems. You'll find Windows is the most common system in use for Office applications.

Take Both Systems

If you really cannot make up your mind, and cost is not the issue, you can run either operating system on a Mac OS X machine, using the Boot Camp utility to dual boot the system, or using a virtual machine product. This will run a range of operating systems, including OS X, Vista and older operating systems such as XP. This approach involves extra software license costs and either the reduced performance due to virtualization or the need to reboot between systems when you require a different application.

In Summary

Macs and PCs perform the same basic computer operations but there are differences in menu items offered, functions are found in different places and the keys and keystrokes used to perform particular operations are different. If you want to work with others, it will be most helpful if you all use the same operating environment, which is most likely to be the PC and Windows.

Don't forget

If you have serious computer enthusiasts among your friends, you may find that they are using one of the Linux operating systems, open software that is distributed without charge. Linux and open software applications are not directly compatible with Mac OS or Windows, but they can be run on PC or Mac systems, via dual boot or virtualization.

Don't forget

Windows also supports dual boot and virtual machine operations. However, Apple does not provide a stand-alone version of the Mac OS X operating system so this cannot be installed on an IBM compatible PC.

Choosing a Laptop

If you need to travel with your PC or need to minimize the space it takes up, you'll be looking for a laptop computer. The primary factor will be the weight – the more mobile you need to be, the lighter the laptop you'll want.

Dell for example, group their laptops into three ranges by weight, and this in turn dictates the monitor sizes offered.

 Ultra Light (< 5lbs)X

The XPS M1330 model is 12.5 by 9.4 ins by 0.9 to 1.3 ins (being slightly wedge shaped), starts off at less than 4lbs, and features a weight-saving solid state disk drive. The screen size is 13.3 ins.

 Light (5 - 7lbs)

For a larger 15.4 ins screen, the XPS M1530 is 14.1 by 10.4 ins by 0.9 to 1.4 ins and weighs 6.8lbs or more.

The Inspiron 1420 (with a 14.1 ins screen) and Inspiron 1520 (15.4 ins screen) can be configured to provide more economical solutions, but there are plenty of options such as case colors, more powerful processors, extra system memory and enhanced graphics.

3 Desktop Replacement (> 7lbs)

For desktop replacements, the more affordable option is the Inspiron 1720 while the XPS M1730 provides the high performance choice. Both feature 17 ins screens, and both can be configured with dual hard drives.

The ultimate desktop replacement is the briefcase style XPS M2010 with its 20 ins screen and its substantial weight of 18.3lbs.

Other Factors

Battery life may range from 2 or 3 hours for the higher powered machines to 7 or more for the lower powered. Supplementary batteries may be available to increase the usable time between recharges.

Most machines will offer a rewritable DVD drive, or perhaps a combination DVD/CD-RW drive, but you are unlikely to find a floppy drive. However, you can usually purchase an add-on USB drive if you still need access to floppy disks.

Desktop Computers

If you don't need a portable computer, you'll find that the desktop options give you much more choice of monitors, processors, graphics, memory, hard drive and optical drives.

Don't forget

You'll usually be able to choose between budget and high-end ranges, in Dell's case Inspiron and XPS for home and home office users.

Narrow Your Selection

⊟ **Product Category**
- ☐ XPS
- ☑ Inspiron

⊟ **Desktop Monitor Size**
- ☐ No Monitor
- ☐ 19" - 20" (Medium)
- ☐ Over 20" (Large)

⊟ **Price**
- ☐ Less than $400
- ☐ $400-$800
- ☐ $800-$1200
- ☐ More than $1200

⊟ **Processor**
- ☐ AMD
- ☐ Intel Core 2 Extreme
- ☐ Intel Core 2 Quad
- ☐ Intel Core 2 Duo
- ☐ Intel Pentium Dual-Core
- ☐ Intel Celeron

⊟ **Operating System**
- ☐ Windows Vista
- ☐ Windows XP

⊟ **Graphics**
- ☐ Integrated
- ☐ Dedicated Graphics - 128 MB
- ☐ Dedicated Graphics - 256 MB
- ☐ Dedicated Graphics - 512 MB
- ☐ Dedicated Graphics - 768 MB

⊟ **Memory**
- ☐ 1GB
- ☐ 2GB
- ☐ 3GB
- ☐ 4GB

⊟ **Hard Drive**
- ☐ 160GB
- ☐ 250GB
- ☐ 320GB
- ☐ 500GB
- ☐ 750GB

⊟ **Optical Drive**
- ☐ CD-RW / DVD-ROM
- ☐ CD/DVD+RW
- ☐ DVD+/-RW and CD-RW Combo
- ☐ DVD-ROM Drive & DVD+/-RW Combo
- ☐ Blu-Ray Disc

Collapse All │ Clear All

To illustrate the options:

1 Select a basic computer such as the Inspiron 530, for email, Internet surfing and documents

2 Choose a higher specification machine such as the XPS 420 for multitasking, playing music, watching videos, running graphics programs or playing games

You can adjust the configuration for the selected model by choosing alternative components such as monitor, graphics card or hard disk. You can also include add-on items such as a TV tuner, networking device, web camera, printer and scanner.

Hot tip

For all but the most basic requirements, choose 2GB memory and a dedicated graphics card with 256MB or more memory installed.

16

All-in-One

To get the space-saving benefits of laptops and the flexible configuration options of the desktop, choose an all-in-one design such as the Dell XPS One.

There's just a monitor on a stand, a wireless keyboard and mouse and a remote control. Everything else is included in the monitor,

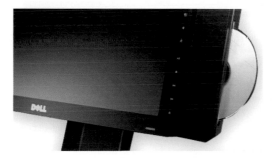

e.g. hard disk, a slot loading CD/DVD re-writer, six USB ports, an 8 in 1 media card reader, audio input/output and TV input.

Hot tip

This incorporates a 20 ins HD (high definition) wide screen monitor with integrated camera and microphone and 10 Watt stereo speakers.

Don't forget

There's a set of touch sensitive buttons on the lower right of the monitor, controlled by a proximity sensor so they only appear when you want to use them.

Don't forget

There is built-in wireless networking, with RF, IR, WiFi and Bluetooth, plus Gigabyte Ethernet.

Help with Selecting

To see how HP provides help for choosing your computer:

We've used Dell to show how you can zero in on the computer that best fits your requirements, but all the suppliers are equally keen to help you find your way through the range of alternatives.

1 Visit **www.hp.com**, select Products & Services, then pick the product type and area, e.g. notebooks for home use

Don't forget

HP offers similar help for choosing desktop computers for home use, and there are also buying guides for the business and large enterprise users.

18

2 You can filter the systems by category, price, brand, display, size, weight and other factors, to select your preference

Hot tip

Apple provide similar assistance to help you choose your Mac or MacBook.

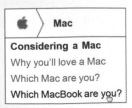

3 For more specific advice, click Help me choose a notebook, then select appropriate answers from any of the panels, to see the recommendations

2 Explore Your Computer

We explore a typical computer, to identify the hardware components involved, the operating system and its features and the additional software including office applications and other useful programs, tools and utilities.

The Example Computer

For the purposes of illustration, we will use a mid range Hewlett Packard DC5800 computer. This is a desktop PC aimed particularly at the small business user, though equally suitable for home and home office use.

This computer includes the following main components:

The Display

This is the HP L1908W 19 ins wide-screen LCD flat panel display with maximum resolution 1440 x 900 pixels.

The Mouse

An HP PS2 style cable-connected 2-button optical scroll wheel mouse.

The keyboard

A standard PS2 style 105 key cable-connected keyboard, in this case with UK keyboard layout.

The System Unit

This can be placed horizontally on the desktop or vertically (like a tower model) though in that case HP recommends the optional tower stand.

Don't forget

Since there is more than 256MB memory assigned to the graphics adapter, this system will support the Windows Aero functions.

The system unit includes a 2.7GHz Intel Core 2 Duo processor, 2GB memory, a 250GB hard disk drive, a DVD/CD re-writer drive and an integrated graphics adapter (which shares part of the main computer memory).

The front panel of the system unit also offers microphone and headphone connectors and a pair of USB ports. In the location that might previously have been assigned to the floppy drive there is a media card reader that supports up to twelve types of memory card, plus a third USB port.

The rear of the unit includes the video VGA connector, the PS2 style mouse and keyboard connectors, a serial port connector, power and audio connectors and a further six USB ports.

Hot tip

There are also slots for up to four hardware adapter cards, though these are not used for the base configuration.

Computer Configuration

When you start up the computer with its Windows Vista operating system, it normally displays the Welcome panel with View Computer Details selected and some basic facts displayed.

1 For more information, click Show More Details

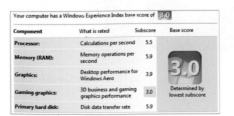

Your computer has a Windows Experience Index base score of 3.0

Component	What is rated	Subscore	Base score
Processor:	Calculations per second	5.5	
Memory (RAM):	Memory operations per second	5.9	
Graphics:	Desktop performance for Windows Aero	3.9	3.0
Gaming graphics:	3D business and gaming graphics performance	3.0	Determined by lowest subscore
Primary hard disk:	Disk data transfer rate	5.9	

The System window shows details such as the processor type, memory and system level. It also shows the system performance rating, in this case a value of 3.0.

1 Select the Device Manager link from the System details

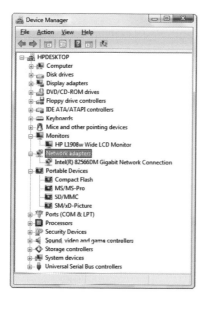

2 Click the plus [+] next to a heading to expand the list, or select and double-click the heading

3 Double-click an entry to view the details of drivers and resources

4 Click the minus [-] next to a heading to collapse the list of entries

5 For an overview of the storage devices defined for the computer, select the Start button and click Computer

6 Drive letters E:, F:, G: and H: are assigned to the media card reader device

Hot tip

The entry for Network Adapters shows that the ethernet adapter has a high speed 1 Gigabit connection.

Hot tip

There are four entries for Portable Devices, reflecting the four slots in the media card reader.

Don't forget

The Computer window also shows the hard disk (drive C:) and the DVD re-writer (drive D:).

23

Activating Vista

When you first use Windows Vista, you are required to Activate your copy. Activation helps verify that your copy of Windows is genuine and that it has not been used on more computers than the Microsoft Software License Terms allow.

You have 30 days after installing Windows to activate it online, or by telephone if there's no Internet connection (see page 25).

Don't forget

If at setup you chose to automatically activate Windows online, this will be carried out three days after you log on for the first time.

1 Click Show More Details from the Welcome Center (see page 22) to display the System window

2 Alternatively, click Start, Computer and then select System Properties

3 Scroll down to Windows Activation, where you can view your activation status

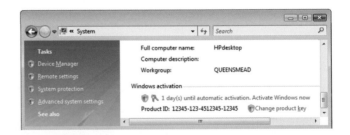

Beware

If you are prompted for an administrator password or confirm the action, you must type the password or provide confirmation before proceeding.

4 If activation is required, select the link to Activate Windows now and click Activate Windows online now

24

5 Activation is initiated, taking a few minutes to complete

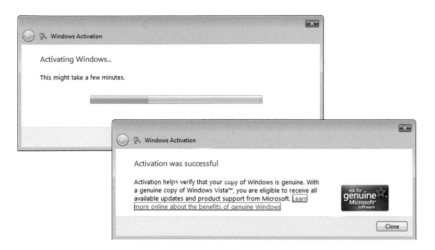

Beware

If you make significant hardware changes, or if you restore your system to a checkpoint prior to activation, you may need to reactivate your copy of Windows Vista.

The status of your Windows activation will be updated.

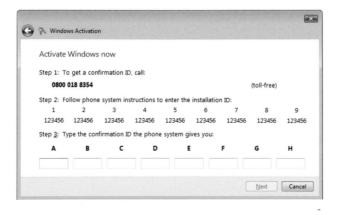

If there's no connection to the Internet, you can choose to activate via a modem, if installed and connected, or by telephone using the automated system and entering installation and confirmation IDs.

Don't forget

Follow the prompts to find the telephone number for your country. You'll need to enter a 54 digit installation ID, and then enter the 48 digit confirmation ID to activate your system.

Operating System Features

The main features of Windows Vista can be found in all of the editions. However there are some features that are included only in the more advanced editions.

Windows Vista	Home Basic	Home Premium	Business	Ultimate
Windows Aero		✓	✓	✓
Windows Meeting Space	Limited	✓	✓	✓
Windows Tablet PC		✓	✓	✓
Windows DVD Maker		✓		✓
Windows Media Center		✓		✓
Windows Movie Maker	✓	✓		✓
Encrypting File System			✓	✓
Integrated smart card management			✓	✓
Group Policy support			✓	✓
Roaming user profiles			✓	✓
Virtual PC Express			✓	✓
Windows BitLocker Drive Encryption				✓
Windows Fax and Scan			✓	✓
Windows ShadowCopy			✓	✓
Windows Ultimate Extras				✓

Make sure that the edition of Windows Vista that you choose supports the features that you will want to use, for example:

Windows Aero
This is in all editions except Basic, and provides an enhanced visual presentation that includes translucency, windows animations and 3D effects (see page 37).

Windows DVD Maker
In Premium and Ultimate editions, you can create professional-looking video DVDs of your home movies and photos and view the results on your DVD player.

Windows Media Center
An all-in-one entertainment center, Media Center is incorporated into Premium and Business editions and allows you to manage photos, music, home videos and television programs.

Windows Ultimate Extras
Exclusive to the Ultimate edition, these add-ons include games, sound schemes, video backgrounds for your desktop and tools to extend the drive encryption capabilities included with Vista.

Programs Included

Windows manages your monitor, mouse and keyboard and all the devices incorporated into your computer. You'll find many of these functions in the Control Panel.

Windows Vista also includes a whole series of programs to help you carry out the tasks that justified your purchase. The main Windows programs and Accessories are displayed in the Start menu (see page 41) and include the following:

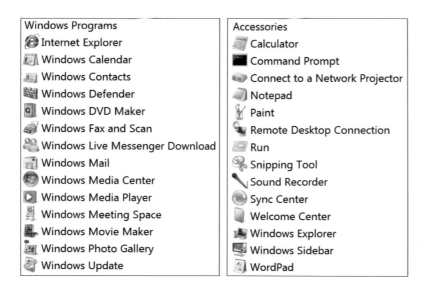

Windows Programs	Accessories
Internet Explorer	Calculator
Windows Calendar	Command Prompt
Windows Contacts	Connect to a Network Projector
Windows Defender	Notepad
Windows DVD Maker	Paint
Windows Fax and Scan	Remote Desktop Connection
Windows Live Messenger Download	Run
Windows Mail	Snipping Tool
Windows Media Center	Sound Recorder
Windows Media Player	Sync Center
Windows Meeting Space	Welcome Center
Windows Movie Maker	Windows Explorer
Windows Photo Gallery	Windows Sidebar
Windows Update	WordPad

The built-in Windows programs provide valuable functions and are ideal for casual use. For more demanding requirements, you should use a full function office package (see pages 29-30).

Don't forget

There are additional programs, tools, utilities, games and functions to be found in other Start menu subfolders.

Ease of Access
System Tools
Tablet PC
Extras and Upgrades
Games
Maintenance
Startup

Microsoft Works

For home and home office use, the Microsoft Works 9.0 package will provide the basic productivity tools you need to prepare documents, control budgets, create greetings cards or manage projects.

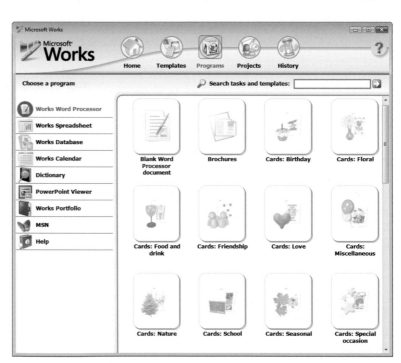

📁 Microsoft Works
📘 Getting Started
📅 Microsoft Works Calendar
📊 Microsoft Works Database
📄 Microsoft Works Portfolio
📈 Microsoft Works Spreadsheet
📝 Microsoft Works Task Launcher
✏️ Microsoft Works Word Processor

1 Click Start, All Programs and select Microsoft Works Task Launcher

2 Click the Programs button and select for example the Works Word Processor then choose the document type

3 Your computer may feature the Works Plus 2008 suite of applications, which includes a copy of Microsoft Office Word 2003, a higher function word processor, in place of the Works word processor

Microsoft Office

For a more robust set of office applications, you'd use Microsoft Office, the latest version being Microsoft Office 2007. There are a number of different editions, each with its own particular selection of applications:

Editions / Applications	Basic	Home & Student	Standard	Small Business	Professional	Ultimate	Professional Plus	Enterprise
Word	Y	Y	Y	Y	Y	Y	Y	Y
Excel	Y	Y	Y	Y	Y	Y	Y	Y
PowerPoint	-	Y	Y	Y	Y	Y	Y	Y
Outlook	Y	-	Y	-	-	-	Y	Y
Outlook + BCM	-	-	-	Y	Y	Y	-	-
Publisher	-	-	-	Y	Y	Y	Y	Y
Access	-	-	-	-	Y	Y	Y	Y
OneNote	-	Y	-	-	-	Y	-	Y
Communicator	-	-	-	-	-	-	Y	Y
InfoPath	-	-	-	-	-	Y	Y	Y
Groove	-	-	-	-	-	Y	-	Y
Project	-	-	-	-	-	-	-	-
SharePoint Designer	-	-	-	-	-	-	-	-
Visio	-	-	-	-	-	-	-	-

Don't forget

Some editions have Outlook alone, while others have Outlook plus Business Contact Manager (BCM).

Hot tip

Some of the Office System applications are only available as individual products, not as part of a suite.

Beware

You'll only see this set of applications if you have the Ultimate edition of Office 2007 installed on your system.

1   Click Start, All Programs and select Microsoft Office to see the applications available

2   Click Microsoft Office Tools to list additional programs and utilities that are provided with Office

Microsoft Office
- Microsoft Office Access 2007
- Microsoft Office Excel 2007
- Microsoft Office Groove 2007
- Microsoft Office InfoPath 2007
- Microsoft Office OneNote 2007
- Microsoft Office Outlook 2007
- Microsoft Office PowerPoint 2007
- Microsoft Office Publisher 2007
- Microsoft Office Word 2007
- Microsoft Office Tools

Adobe Reader

There's a huge variety of software available for Windows-based computers, tailored to meet particular needs and requirements. Many such products can be downloaded from the Internet, often at no charge. Here are some that will prove particularly useful:

 Go to the web page **www.adobe.com** and click the Get Adobe Reader button

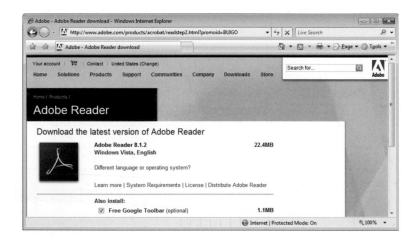

You can clear the box for the Google Toolbar which is not a requirement for use of Adobe Reader

Scroll down, click the Download Now button, then follow the prompts to download, install and configure the Reader

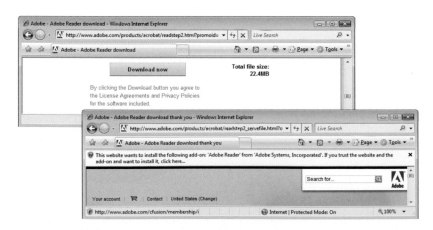

AVG Antivirus

There is a free edition of the AVG Antivirus program that
provides protection from file corruption programs.

1 At website free.grisoft.com click the Get It Now button
for free basic protection, the AVG Antivirus free edition

2 Click the Continue to AVG Free Download button

Continue to AVG Free download

3 Follow the prompts to download and install the AVG
antivirus program

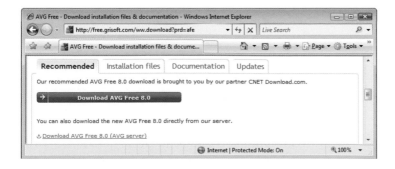

Don't forget

The AVG Antivirus Free
Edition provides basic
antivirus and anti-
spyware protection for
Windows, for home and
non-commercial use.

Hot tip

You can download from
the CNET download.com
website or directly from
the AVG server. The file
size is around 50 MB.

Don't forget

Once installed, AVG will
automatically apply the
latest updates, and will
refresh the data files on
a daily basis.

IrfanView

The third recommended application is the IrfanView graphic viewer. This is a small, compact and very fast freeware application for non-commercial use which runs under most versions of Windows, Vista included.

1 Go to website **www.irfanview.com** and click the link to download the current version of IrfanView

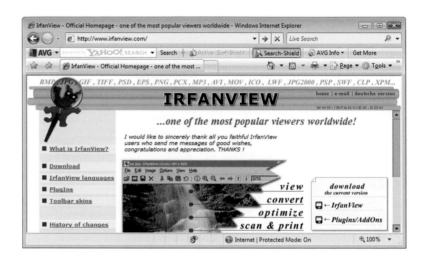

2 This application is also available from the CNET website **download.com**. Click the Download Now link

 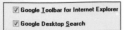

3 Follow the prompts to complete the installation and launch the IrfanView program

3 Windows Basics

Here we look more closely at Windows Vista and the ways in which you can control its appearance and manage the systems and applications windows. The differences between Windows Vista Basic and Windows Vista Aero are explained. Finally, we look at the types of user accounts that Windows provides and how you add new users.

Beware

If your system has Windows Aero enabled, you'll see special visual effects such as transparency. However, the illustrations in the book generally use the Windows Vista Basic effects.

Hot tip

This illustrates the display when you have two active Windows applications e.g. WordPad and Paint.

Hot tip

A tick (✓) is applied to the Quick Launch entry to show that it is active. Click a second time to remove the tick and hide the Quick Launch bar.

Windows Display

What you see on your computer depends on which version of Windows you have installed, the updates that have been applied and any customization that has been carried out. So don't be surprised if things are not exactly the same as illustrated here.

However, the differences are more in the appearance than in how Windows behaves. All versions of Windows use the same basic skills and approaches, though things may vary in their effects and details may be rearranged.

There are two main sections – the desktop and the taskbar.

The Desktop

Icons and Shortcuts   Desktop Area   Application Windows   Windows Sidebar

Start Button   Quick Launch Bar   Taskbar with Tasks   Notification Area

The Taskbar

If the Quick Launch toolbar doesn't show on your system:

1 Right-click the Taskbar, select Toolbars and then select the Quick Launch entry

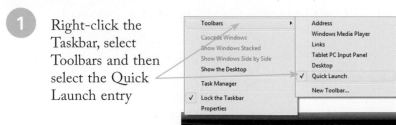

Background

There's usually a picture or image shown as the background to the desktop. You can change this to something more personal.

1 Right-click an empty area on the desktop and select Personalize

2 Select the Desktop Background entry then select the location from which to choose a background

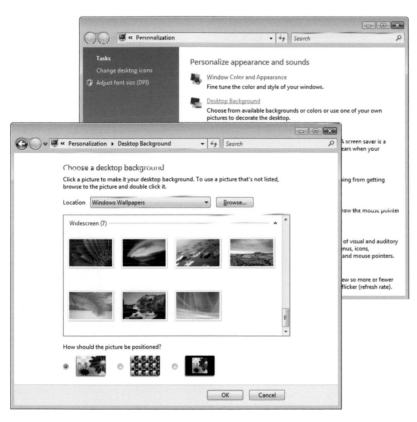

3 Select an image and it is applied immediately

4 You can fit the screen, or tile the screen with multiple copies or simply center the image on the screen

5 Click OK to complete the process

Screen Resolution

The screen resolution governs the clarity and the size of the screen contents. At higher resolutions (e.g. 1440 x 720) items are smaller and sharper, and more items can be displayed. At low resolutions (e.g. 800 x 600) items appear larger, fewer items can be displayed and the overall image may appear less precise.

To adjust the screen resolution:

1 From the Personalize panel, select Display Settings

2 Drag the slider to choose your preferred display resolution

For an LCD monitor, choose the native resolution (usually the highest). For a CRT, choose the highest resolution that will give you 32 bit color and at least 72 Hertz refresh rate.

1 To check the refresh rate for the selected resolution, click Advanced Settings and select Monitor

2 Click the arrow to view the alternatives

Appearance

You can change the way the desktop appears.

1 From Personalize, select Windows Color and Appearance

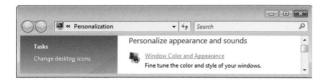

2 If Windows Aero is active, this panel is displayed

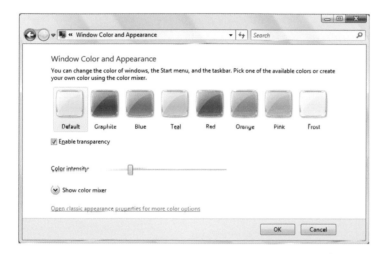

Hot tip

This panel isn't available if your graphics hardware does not support Windows Aero.

3 Select Open classic appearance properties for more color options

4 Switch between Windows Aero, Windows Vista Basic, Windows Standard and Windows Classic

5 Click OK to apply any selected changes

Don't forget

This is the panel that appears when you select Windows Color and Appearance without Windows Aero active.

Mouse Settings

You can change the way that the mouse pointer appears and how it behaves when clicking and selecting.

1 From the Personalization panel select Mouse Pointers

2 Click the Pointers tab to choose a mouse pointer scheme, to enable or disable pointer shadows and to customize specific pointers

38

3 Click the Buttons tab to exchange the primary and secondary (left and right) buttons, to check and adjust the double-click speed and to turn on the ClickLock option

4 Click the Pointer Options tab to adjust the pointer speed and to enhance the pointer precision

Don't forget

Adjusting the pointer speed translates mouse movements across the mouse mat into greater or lesser pointer movements across the screen.

5 Click the SnapTo box to automatically move the mouse pointer to the default button when you open a dialog box

6 You can help keep track of the position of the mouse pointer by enabling pointer trails, or by choosing to show the pointer location when you press the Ctrl key

Hot tip

Pressing Ctrl displays a series of decreasing circles that zero onto the mouse pointer location.

7 Click the Wheel tab to review or change actions using the mouse wheel (if there's one fitted on your mouse)

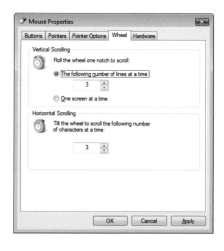

Don't forget

Click the Hardware tab to review the device details and click the Properties button to change the hardware settings.

Properties

Starting Windows

When you turn on your computer, the system initializes and then displays the Logon screen, with the user names that are defined.

 Click on the user name required for this session

 Type the associated password and press the Enter key (or click the arrow) to display the Windows desktop

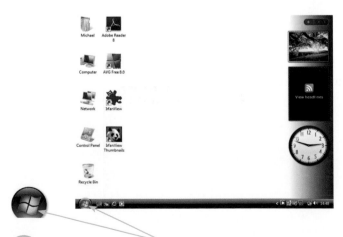

 Click the Start button to display the Start Menu

Start Menu

Predefined Programs   Recently Used Programs   Picture for Selected item (or user account)

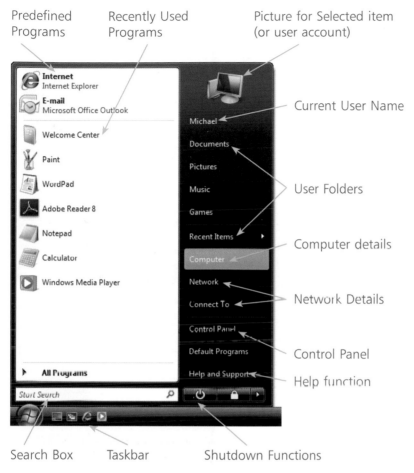

Current User Name

User Folders

Computer details

Network Details

Control Panel

Help function

Search Box   Taskbar   Shutdown Functions

Hot tip

You can also display the Start Menu by pressing one of the Windows Logo keys, found next to the Ctrl keys on the keyboard.

The Shutdown functions provide options to turn off your computer, temporarily or fully, or to switch user names etc.

1 Click Start and then click the Power button to turn off your computer

Switch User
Log Off
Lock

Restart

Sleep
Shut Down

2 Click the Lock button to leave your computer in a secure state

3 Click the arrow next to the Lock button to switch users, log off the current user name, shutdown and restart or shutdown completely

Don't forget

By default, Windows places the computer into an energy-saving Sleep mode which automatically saves your open documents and turns off all non-essential functions. When you restart, it returns quickly to where you left off.

Open a Window

1. Select one of the fixed links, one of the recently used programs or a folder, from the list at the top level of the Start Menu (see page 41)

2. Click All Programs, then scroll through the menus, clicking submenus to open them if necessary. Locate and select the required entry

3. Type part of the name into the Search box and select the desired program, folder or file from the list of matches that gets displayed

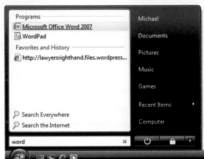

4. Select a shortcut entry from the Quick Launch bar

5. Double-click an icon in a folder or on the desktop, to open a window with the associated program

6. Right-click a file in a folder or on the desktop, select Open With and choose a suitable application from the list offered

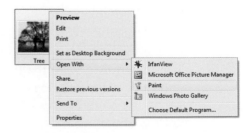

Window Structures

When you open a folder it opens a window that displays the contents of that folder as file or folder icons. Programs open as windows that are specific to the particular application. There will be differences but the windows share many features in common.

Folder Window

Forward and Back | Folder Path | Search Box | Minimize Maximize/Restore

Close

Title Bar Area

Command Bar

Scroll Bar

File Icons

Navigation Pane

Details Pane

Hot tip

These file icons are in the form of Thumbnail icons (miniature images). Click the Views button to switch between List, Details and Tile icons.

43

Program/File Window

Right-click a picture file icon and open it with a suitable program, in this case Windows Paint. You will find that this application window uses the Title bar at the top. Below this is the Menu bar. There's also a toolbar and a color palette. There are two scroll bars since the picture is larger than the available image area.

Don't forget

This illustrates the fact that some applications preserve the windows style from Windows XP, witness the menu bar, while other applications will use the updated Windows Vista styling.

Move and Resize Windows

To reposition a folder or application window on the screen:

1 Move the mouse pointer over the title bar, then click and drag the window to the required location

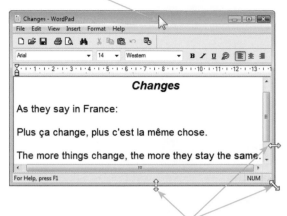

2 Click and drag an edge to resize the window horizontally or vertically, or click a corner to resize in two directions

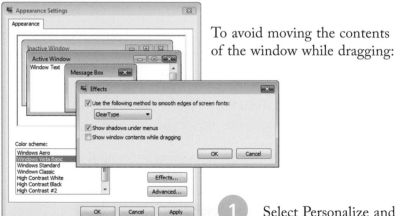

To avoid moving the contents of the window while dragging:

1 Select Personalize and Windows Color and Appearance, click the Effects button, clear the Show Window Contents box, then click OK and Apply

Select a Window (Basic)

When you have numerous windows open on your desktop, you
need functions to help you switch to the one you want next.

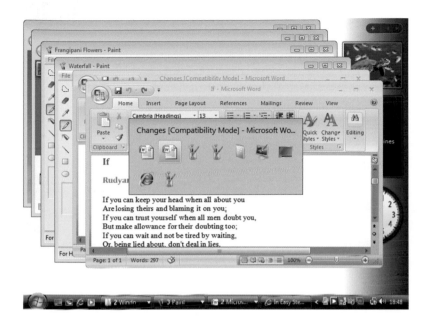

Hot tip

One of the entries is for
the desktop itself, which
provides another way to
minimize all the windows
on the desktop.

1 Press Alt+tab or click the Switch Between Windows
button on the Quick Launch bar and choose a window

2 Pause the mouse pointer over an entry on the taskbar
and the full program and document names are shown

Don't forget

When there are multiple
entries on the taskbar,
Windows may group
three or more items of
the same type together
to save space.

3 If there are multiple tasks grouped together, click the
group and the individual items are displayed

4 Click any entry on the taskbar to switch to that window

Select a Window (Aero)

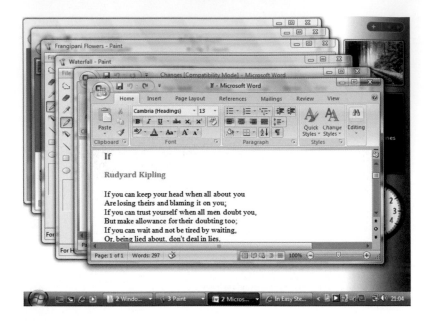

Don't forget

If your system has the Aero feature active, the window selection functions will operate somewhat differently.

Hot tip

This panel contains thumbnails of the open windows, and just icons for windows that are minimized to the taskbar. See page 47 for the actions of Switch Between Windows when Aero is enabled.

1 Press Alt+tab and choose a window

2 Pause the mouse pointer over an entry on the taskbar and a thumbnail of the window is shown

Don't forget

These are dynamic thumbnail images, so they will reflect realtime changes to the window contents.

3 If there are multiple tasks grouped together, click the group and the individual items are displayed. Pause over an entry in the group to see its thumbnail image

4 Press the Switch Between Windows button on the Quick Launch bar and the open windows are displayed in a stack format known as Flip 3D

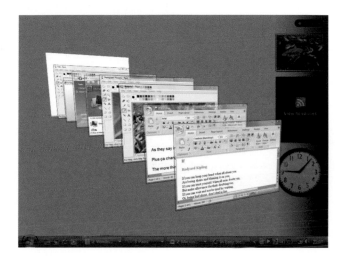

5 Press Windows Logo key plus Tab successively to flip through the set of windows, one by one

6 When the required window is at the front, select the Switch Between Windows button, or click on that window and it becomes the current window

Close a Window

There are a number of different ways to close windows when you have finished with them. To close a specific window:

1 Select the window to make it the active window, and then click the Close button to the right on the title bar

2 This works the same under Windows Aero and Windows Vista Basic, though the appearance may differ.

You can also close the window from the taskbar.

1 Right-click the entry on the taskbar and select Close from the menu

2 For a group of items, right-click the group and select Close Group

If any of the windows contain modified files, you'll be prompted to save them before continuing on to close the windows

New User Account

You'll need an extra user account if your main user account has been set up with full administrator privileges. You may also need accounts for other users of the computer, to help keep your emails and documents separate. To add an account:

Hot tip

You could also double-click Add New Users in Welcome Center to open the user accounts area.

1 Select Start, Control Panel and click User Accounts and Family Safety

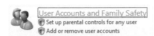

2 Select the entry to Add or remove user accounts

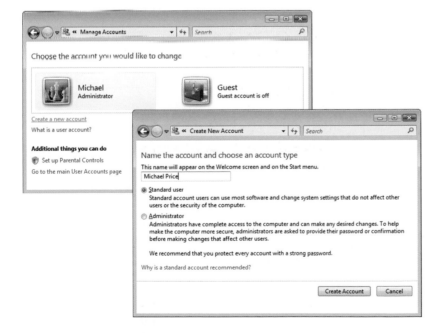

Don't forget

You can enable the more restrictive Guest account for casual users of your computer.

Hot tip

Make sure you know the password for your Administrator level account, since this is often all that's needed to confirm authority for system tasks.

3 Provide the account name and choose the account type. This should normally be Standard, although you do need an Administrator account for system actions

...cont'd

Don't forget

If you have an administrator account, you can change the settings, including passwords, for any user on the computer.

4   To make changes to the settings, click on the new entry

5   You can change the account name, picture or type, and you can also Create a password

Don't forget

If you sign on using a standard account, you can only modify the password and the picture associated with that account. Any other actions will require an administrator account ID and password

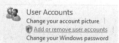

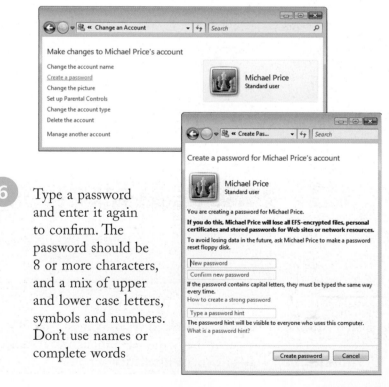

6   Type a password and enter it again to confirm. The password should be 8 or more characters, and a mix of upper and lower case letters, symbols and numbers. Don't use names or complete words

4 Word Processing

Use your word processor to create letters, memos and reports. Add interest and emphasis to your documents by using different fonts and adding illustrations. Learn the basic skills and to use the standard tools provided in the word processor, which can be transferred to other applications. For example, add pictures and clip art, or use templates for documents.

Word Processors

Word processing is a basic computer function. It has been a feature since PCs first came in to being, but has grown dramatically in functionality and ease of use. It can be used to create anything from a simple memo through to a complex manuscript, complete with illustrations, indexes and footnotes.

Notepad
Supplied with all versions of Windows, this is a basic text processor. It enables you to create and save generic

Notepad
Creates and edits text files using basic text formatting

text documents that have no formatting and so can be read by virtually any word processor. Notepad documents are used by many software manufacturers to create soft copy manuals and instruction booklets and have the file suffix .txt.

WordPad
WordPad is a limited function word processor, also included with all editions of Windows. If all you wished to do was

WordPad
Creates text documents with complex formatting

create simple documents with some degree of layout and font enhancements, it would be sufficient.

Word
Included in all versions of Microsoft Office, Word is a full function word processor. With this program you can

Microsoft Office Word
Creates professional-looking documents such as letters, papers and reports

create professional documents, add indexes, captions and tables of figures. You can specify languages and dictionaries, insert standard text and bibliographies.

Microsoft Works
This is the 'lite' version of Office, often installed on home computers. The Works Suite version includes Word

Works Word Processor
Create letters, reports and other documents

as supplied with Office. The standard version includes the Works word processor which is a mid-function application that is more than sufficient for most purposes, particularly in the home environment.

Create a Document

Although we are using Word to illustrate the word processing window, all the word processors mentioned on the previous page will appear very similar and behave much the same when simply entering text.

1 When you open the word processor you will see the cursor flashing at the start of the document, indicating the point where the typing will begin

2 The text will automatically wrap to the next line as you type

3 Press Enter (the carriage return key) when you wish to start a new paragraph

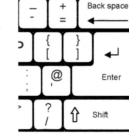

4 Press the Caps Lock key to get all capitals or the Shift key to get individual capitals

5 Press the Shift key to get the character shown on the top of the key, even when the Caps Lock key is on

Hot tip

When you open Word the Home tab is selected, providing access to the most used functions such as font formats, text alignments and editing facilities.

Don't forget

All the keys are typomatic (repeating). This also applies to the spacebar, which is treated as a character like any other.

Don't forget

The numeric keypad on the right of the keyboard, has two functions – numbers and navigation. To get numbers, the Num Lock key indicator must be lit.

Layout Your Page

Your word processor has certain settings already defined. These are known as the default settings and include such items as font styles and sizes and the page layout options such as margins, line spacing and page orientation.

To change the page layout:

1 Select the Page Layout tab and click the Margins option. Several standard settings are offered, including narrow, wide and mirrored margins

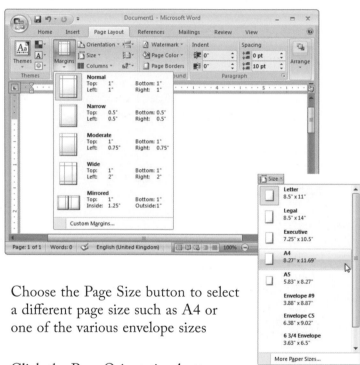

2 Choose the Page Size button to select a different page size such as A4 or one of the various envelope sizes

3 Click the Page Orientation button to change the page from the default Portrait to Landscape

4 Select the View tab and tick the Ruler box to view the horizontal ruler at the top of the typing area

54

Navigate the Document

In normal typing mode Word can only display a screenful of typing at a time. You can use the following methods to move around the document:

1 Press the Home key to move the cursor to the left margin and the End key to move to the end of the line

2 Press the Ctrl+Home keys together (press the Ctrl key first) to move swiftly to the beginning of the document and Ctrl+End to move to the end of the document

3 Press the Page Down key to move down a screenful of text and the Page Up key to do the reverse

4 Select the View tab to access functions such as Zoom the document or view one or two whole pages at once

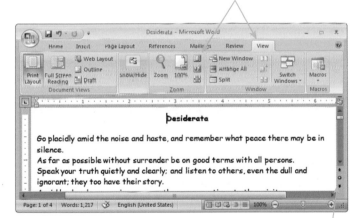

5 Use the Page Navigation icons to move through the document one page at a time

6 On the Home tab, click Find and Go To, to specify a particular page, useful with long documents

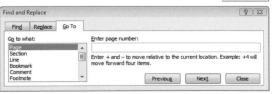

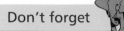

Don't forget

If you have a mouse with a scrolling wheel, you can use that to scroll through the document.

Hot tip

Use the Zoom slider located on the bottom of the window frame as an alternative

Hot tip

The bottom left frame of the window indicates the number of pages and number of words in the document.

Save the Document

With several lines of text created, save the document, currently named the default Document 1, to your hard disk.

1 Click the Office button and select Save. Alternatively click the Save button on the Quick Access toolbar. The first time you save the file, Word opens the Save As window

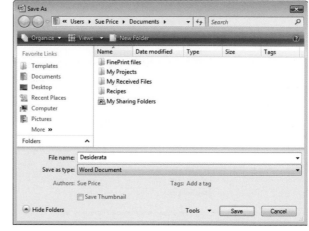

2 The file will be saved into the Documents folder and the first line of the file is selected as the file name, in this case Desiderata

3 The Word Titlebar now shows the name of the file, indicating that it has been successfully saved

4 When you next save the file, repeat the same procedure. The existing file will be overwritten with your additions and amendments without further prompting

Save Options

To save the file as a new version with a different name:

1 Click the Office button and select Save As

2 Choose to save it as a Word document and you can now change the file name

You can also change the destination drive or folder:

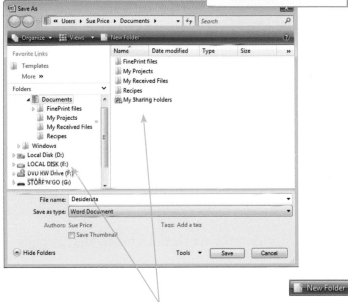

1 Double-click a different drive or folder in the folder list or click New Folder in the Toolbar

2 Name the new folder and press Enter. This creates and immediately opens the new folder for you to use

To save in a version that is compatible with older versions of Word:

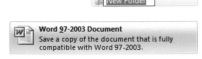

1 Click the Word 97-2003 option or select Other Formats for a full range of options

Hot tip

If you wish to share a file with others who have previous versions of Office, it is essential to save the file as an older version. The default version of an Office 2007 file is unreadable by older applications.

Revise the Text

1. Open your file, if necessary, by selecting the Office button and click Open or press Ctrl+O

2. Double-click the file name or single click and Open

Word, as the example word processor, always opens in 'insert' mode, so new text added between words will be inserted and automatically push the existing text along.

- Use the Backspace key to remove text to the left of the cursor
- Use the Delete key to delete text to the right of the cursor
- Red wavy lines indicate spelling queries
- Green wavy lines indicate grammar problems

Autocorrect

As you type certain corrections take place automatically, such as reversal of 'teh' to 'the' and capitalization at the beginning of a new sentence. To view the Autocorrect and Autotype options:

1. Click the Office button, Word Options and Proofing

2. Click Autocorrect Options to see more details

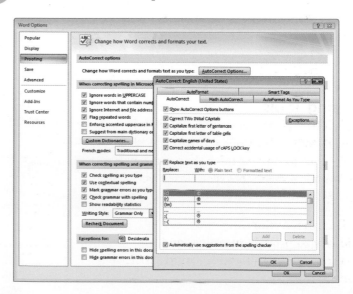

Hot tip

On previous versions of Word you could switch between Insert mode and Replace mode by pressing the Insert key. To activate this function in Word 2007, right-click the Status bar and select Overtype. The option will be added to the Status bar. Click the button to switch.

Overtype

Check Spelling

1 Position the cursor anywhere within the text area, choose the Review tab and click Spelling and Grammar

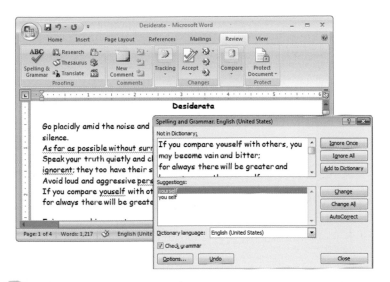

Don't forget

The spell checker will not highlight words spelled correctly but in the wrong context, for example 'form' instead of 'from', or 'piece' instead of 'peace'.

2 The upper pane shows the incorrect spelling in context, with suggestions in the lower pane

Hot tip

The Grammar check will highlight extra spaces between words, incorrect punctuation and potential capitalization.

3 Click Change to accept the spelling correction or Ignore. For technical terms, place names etc. which you use often, you can Add to Dictionary

4 Grammar problems are more subjective and concern writing style so you may wish to choose Ignore rule

Proofing Tools

Word 2007 has extensive dictionary and language tools. Options include translating into Arabic, French and Spanish. You can hover over a word and instantly translate it to your chosen language.

The Research option uses the Encarta dictionary to provide meanings and the Thesaurus to offer alternative words, including antonyms.

Move and Copy Text

You can move or copy text within the same document, to another Word document or to another application. Text selected in an application, then cut or copied, is stored temporarily by the computer in an area called the Clipboard.

To copy or move text, you must first select it. You can use any of the following methods:

1 Position the mouse in the left margin so that it points towards the text. Click to select the line, or keep the mouse button held down and drag down the screen to select more. The text will be highlighted

60

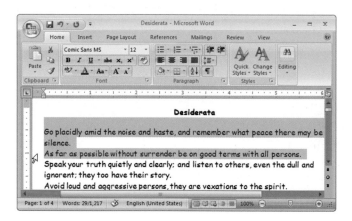

2 Double-click on a single word to select just the word, or triple click to select the paragraph

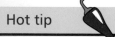
3 Click at the beginning of the desired text, then press and hold the Shift key and click at the end of the text

4 With the Home tab selected, click Select on the Editing command. This offers further options for more complex actions such as selecting objects in the background

To Move Text

1 Select the text and on the Home tab click the Cut icon. The text will disappear from the window

2 Position the cursor where you wish to place the text and click the Paste icon

To Copy Text

1 Select the text and click the Copy icon. This time the text will remain in the window

2 Reposition the cursor and click Paste

Office Clipboard

This facility enables you to collect multiple clips and rearrange your document more easily. It holds up to 24 items and can be used to copy text, tables or images between Office applications. Open Excel or PowerPoint and the Office Clipboard to see your Word clips. To activate it:

1 Click the small arrow next to Clipboard on the Command bar

2 As you cut or copy the text it will appear in the Clipboard Manager

3 Position the cursor where you wish to paste the text and click on the item

4 Click the down arrow on an item to Paste or Delete

Hot tip

As an alternative, right-click within the highlighted text and from the Context menu select Cut or Copy. Reposition the cursor, right-click again and select Paste.

Hot tip

The keyboard shortcuts for these actions are:
Ctrl+X to cut
Ctrl+C to copy
Ctrl+V to paste
These shortcuts work with all the word processors listed on page 52.

61

Don't forget

Click the Options button to enable the Office Clipboard automatically.

Add Format and Style

Text created in a new Word document is formatted as 'Normal' text. This means that it has specific attributes of font face and size applied by Word. To alter the font:

1 Select the text to change and on the Home tab, click the arrow next to the font face or font size

2 Word 2007 has a preview facility that immediately illustrates the effect of the change

3 The Bold, Italic and Underline tools are toggle switches. Select the text to be formatted and click the required effect. Click again to reverse the action. You can apply one or all of the effects to the selected text

Alignment

Text in the document is automatically aligned to the left margin. To change its position:

1 Simply click within the paragraph you wish to realign and click: Left   Center   Right   Justified

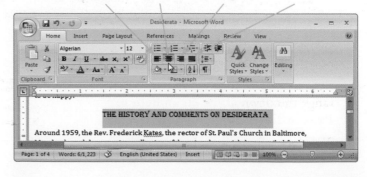

Hot tip

Using the alignment buttons means that if you change the document margins, the text will still be correctly positioned.

Don't forget

The Alignment buttons are not toggle switches – one alignment button is always selected.

Format Painter

This tool offers a swift way to copy font format, such as font face, size and attributes including emphasis and alignment.

1 With the Home tab selected, click in the text with the required formatting and then single click the Format Painter tool

2 Move to the target text and click. The format will be applied

3 To apply the format to several areas of text, double-click Format Painter and then click on the tool when finished

Style Options

Word offers a number of style templates. The Normal template is selected when you open the application. To apply a different style:

1 Select all or part of the document and pass your mouse over each of the Quick Style options. The Preview feature, new to Office 2007, will illustrate the effect

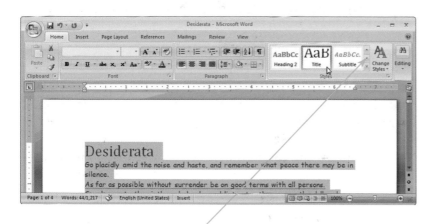

2 Click the up and down arrows to scroll to see further style effects, or click the More button to reveal the full range of options

3 To select a Style, just click on it

Hot tip

Click Change Styles to see an expanded list of style templates, including reverting to Word 2003 style. Use Change Styles to change the default style for all future documents.

Add a Picture

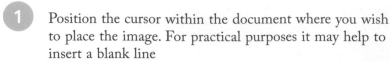

Hot tip

When a picture is selected, Picture Tools appears over the Format tab. Click the tab to access the various tools.

Don't forget

Word has a large range of picture frames and effects that also give an instant preview.

1. Position the cursor within the document where you wish to place the image. For practical purposes it may help to insert a blank line

2. Click the Insert tab, and then Picture. Locate the picture and click Insert

3. Click the Position button for an instant preview of various positioning effects

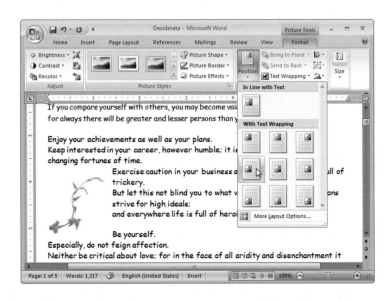

4. Use the Text Wrapping button for more control of the picture's location. Try options such as Square, Tight or Through and drag the picture to the required position

5. To resize the picture, click the up and down buttons on the height. The width will be changed proportionally

6. Click the Rotate option to flip the image, or the green rotation handle for freehand rotation

Use Clip Art

Microsoft Office provides a collection of Clip Art images that can be used to illustrate and add interest to your documents.

1 On the Insert tab, click the Clip Art icon to open the Clip Art search

2 Type your keyword, then choose the search options:
All Collections is made up of My Collections, Office Collections and Web Collections.
All Media File types, which are Clip Art, Photographs, Movies and Sound.

3 When you select the Go button, the Clip Organizer will search through the specified collections and assemble appropriate clips

4 Scroll through the results to choose a clip

5 Position the cursor in the document where you wish the clip to appear and then click on it

6 Once inserted, the clip can be repositioned in exactly the same way as a picture

7 You can resize clip art and images by dragging the frame, but be sure to drag the corner handle to keep the correct proportions

8 Choose Organize Clips to open the Microsoft Clip Organizer. This lists all the categories of clips stored on your computer and allows you to scroll through and view the full range

Hot tip

To view the Web collections, you must have an Internet connection.

Don't forget

Animated clips can only be viewed in Html or web documents.

Don't forget

The majority of clip art picture files in Office are .wmf files. This is a Microsoft vector file format that means that images can be resized without loss of detail.

Print the Document

To print the document

1 Click the Office button and move the arrow to the Print command

Use Print Preview to manage the document layout before printing.

2 Select Print Preview to see the document in its entirety before it is printed

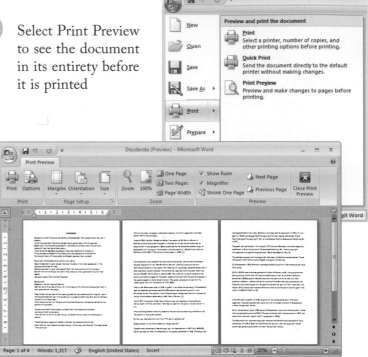

The Print Preview window has the standard Page Setup options which let you adjust the margins, orientation and paper size.

3 Use the Zoom function in Print Preview to see up to six pages at a time

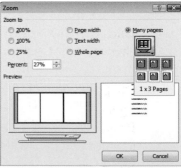

4 Select the Print button on the Preview window to open the Print dialog window as shown on the next page

5 Select Close Print Preview to return to the editing view

Close Print Preview

For full access to the print controls click the first item on the Print menu. With the Print Dialog window open:

Print
Select a printer, number of copies, and other printing options before printing.

1 Choose a printer if there is more than one available

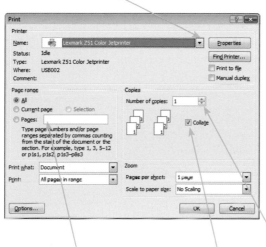

2 Select which pages to print, in which order and how many copies

3 Click OK to start the printing

To add the Quick Print button to the Quick Access toolbar:

1 Click the Customise button and choose More Commands

2 Click Quick Print, Add and then OK

Advanced Documents

Microsoft Word offers a whole range of document templates for standard office documents including letters, faxes and reports. They are displayed in style groups such as Equity, Median and Oriel. There are also templates for more complicated layouts such as brochures, greeting cards and business cards. To view:

1 Click the Office button and select New

2 Installed templates are Microsoft standard, but you can create your own, for example a letterhead or use those available from Office Online

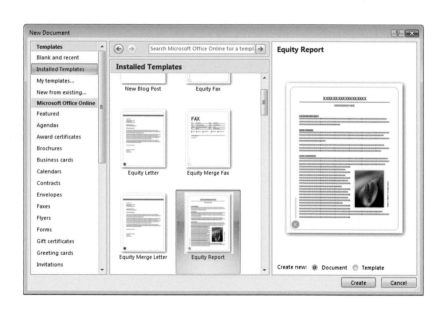

Review, Mailings and References

View the tools and commands on all these tabs within Word to see the extensive range of functions and options that you can use to create and manage complex word processor documents.

● Combine reports, track changes and accept or reject amendments with the Review tools

● Use Mail merge to create bulk mailings of letters, envelopes and labels, using criteria to choose recipients

● Use the References tab to help create a composite document with index, table of contents, captions and bibliographies

5 Communication

Communicating with others using your computer is one of its most useful functions. It is speedy, efficient and cheaper than regular mail. You can contact individuals or whole groups, request receipts to ensure the message has been received and add automatic signatures. Use Instant Messaging software to chat to people all over the world, with a web camera perhaps.

Email

Email, electronic mail, has the advantage of speed together with the benefits of the written word to support your communication. You can reply to the sender, forward to others and send the same email to whole groups of people. While email has its own conventions, it doesn't have the same formality as regular correspondence.

What you need

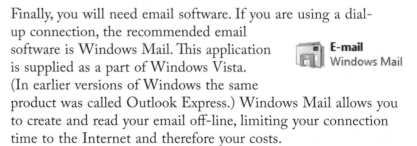

Firstly you need a means to connect to the Internet. This could be a dial-up modem, usually supplied with your computer as a standard fitment, or a broadband router. This is a separate piece of hardware that is usually broadband supplier specific.

Secondly you will need an Internet Service Provider (ISP) and ISP account. Your ISP sign-on will provide you with your primary email address, for example:

sue.price14@btinternet.com

Finally, you will need email software. If you are using a dial-up connection, the recommended email software is Windows Mail. This application is supplied as a part of Windows Vista. (In earlier versions of Windows the same product was called Outlook Express.) Windows Mail allows you to create and read your email off-line, limiting your connection time to the Internet and therefore your costs.

 E-mail Windows Mail

With a broadband connection, you can choose to use either Windows Mail or web-based email. Most ISPs support both methods of accessing your email account. There are also some Internet only email accounts such as Microsoft Hotmail or Googlemail. You access Internet mail using your Internet browser, see page 92.

Whichever software you use, Windows Mail or web-based, the appearance, facilities and processes are very similar. As Windows Mail is included in Vista it is used for the illustrations and processes in this chapter, switching to an alternative is very straightforward.

Don't forget

The broadband router will connect to your computer via the USB port or Ethernet connection.

Don't forget

You can create and use other email addresses, both for yourself and for other users of your computer. See page 49.

Hot tip

Using Windows Mail, your email is stored on your own computer. Web-based mail is stored on the email server and can be accessed from any computer with the correct sign-on.

Create an Account

Your ISP may provide you with a CD to help you register for an account. This will make an initial connection to the Internet where you can provide your personal details and create an account. For example, to register for an account at BT Internet:

1 Sign on to BT Internet and select your account type

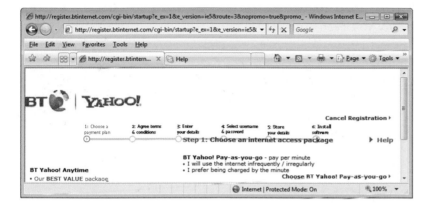

2 Follow the on-screen prompts to agree the terms and conditions and enter your personal details

3 At Step 4 on the progress bar choose your username and password

4 Finally, install the software to complete the account setup

Hot tip

Your computer may also be supplied with pre-installed software for accessing an ISP.

Don't forget

In this example a username is suggested for you, or you can try to create your own. However, the most popular and common usernames will usually be already assigned, so you may have to choose something slightly obscure.

Hot tip

The downloaded software will assign the user name and password for Internet connection, and create your email address in Windows Mail.

Receive Email

1 Click the Windows button and select Windows Mail

2 Click Send/Receive. If you need to connect via your dial-up modem, you will be prompted with a connection window. With a broadband (DSL) connection active, any messages should be directly downloaded to your computer from the ISP server

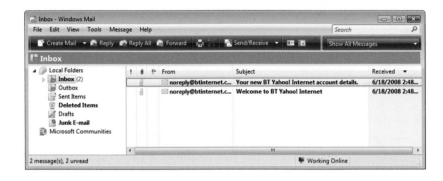

3 The messages are saved into your Inbox and show the sender, subject, date and time

4 In the Folder list on the left of the window, the number in brackets (2) indicates the number of new/unread messages

5 Double-click the message to open and read it. Click the Close button when finished

6 Unread messages are indicated by bolder text and an unopened envelope

Send Email

1 With Windows Mail open, click the Create Mail button to open the New Message window

2 Type the recipient's email address in the To field. If the recipient's email address is in your Contacts list, see page 78, the address will be completed for you

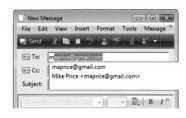

3 To accept the address just press Enter. Continue typing if you require a different recipient or address

4 Complete the Cc line of the email header to send a courtesy copy or carbon copy of the email

5 Click in the Subject line and type your message topic then click in the main area and type your email

6 When finished click the Send button. The message will be moved to your Outbox, which will then indicate the number of messages waiting to be sent

7 The message(s) will stay there until you click on Send/Receive, or until your system does an automatic Send/Receive

8 A copy of the email will also be saved into your Sent Items folder

Reply and Forward

Don't forget

Using the Reply feature ensures that both correspondents are aware of the contents of the original message.

To reply to an incoming email:

1 Select or open the message and click the Reply button. The address line is automatically completed and Re: will be added to the Subject line

2 The cursor will be positioned at the top of the message area, ready for you to type your message. Click Send when completed

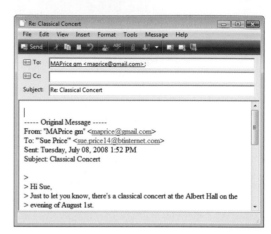

Don't forget

When using Reply, any attachments will be stripped from the email. If you Forward the message, then the attachments remain. See page 76 for working with attachments.

3 The original message in your Inbox indicates that you have replied

4 Use Reply All to respond to all the people who received the original message

To forward a message:

1 Select or open the message and click Forward. This time you must complete the To: field in the message header

2 Fw: is added to the Subject line. Click in the text area to add your own message

3 Click Send when finished

Email Options

To control the Send and Receive functions on your email account.

1 In the main Windows Mail window, select Tools, Options and the General tab

2 Choose options such as to Send and Receive on Startup and how frequently to check for messages

Don't forget

Email text can be plain text or Rich text (html). It's a good idea to choose to send mail in plain text. Many companies are wary of email that contains formatted text and will block them from their systems.

Sending and receiving in plain text will prevent the embedding of attached pictures within the message. Use Rich text when you need to send tables or such data.

3 Click the Read tab and tick the box to Read all messages in plain text. This is the preferred option for greater security

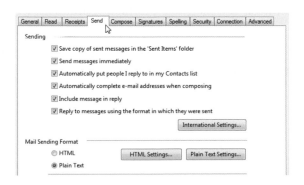

4 On the Send tab, you can see a whole range of features that enable you to customize Windows Mail to your personal requirements

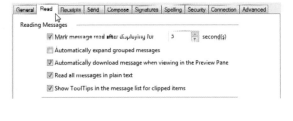

Hot tip

Replying to messages in the format they were sent is the polite option.

75

Attachments

An attachment is a file created outside of the email program. It could be in one of many formats such as a photograph, text document, spreadsheet or scanned document.

To send an attachment with your email:

Beware

Attachments cause concern as they may contain viruses. Do not open them if they are from an unknown source. See page 31 for virus checking.

1 Create your email message, then click the Attach button

2 The Documents folder will open for you to select the required file. If the file is in a different location, you will need to navigate your folders to find it

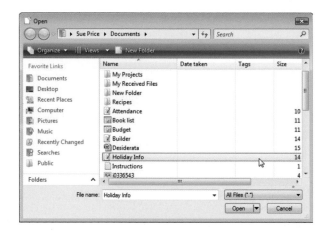

Don't forget

You should be aware of the size of the file when sending attachments. It will be indicated in the Attach line of the header. Large files, in particular photograph files, can take a long time to send and/or be received on a dial-up connection. Some photo programs, such as Microsoft's Photo Premium 10, have a facility that will reduce the file size for emailing as an attachment.

3 Select the file or files and click Open. The message header will display a new field with the name of the attached file

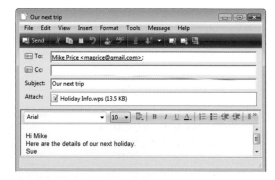

4 Click Send and the message will be transferred to the Outbox

When you receive an email with an attachment:

1 The attachment will be scanned by your virus checker before it is downloaded if you use web-based email, or as it is downloaded for PC based mail

2 The attachment is indicated by the paperclip symbol in the header

3 Open the message and click File, Save attachments

4 Note where the attachment will be saved. The norm is Documents, but if you have used a different folder previously, Windows Mail will remember and suggest that as the destination folder

5 Click Browse to use a different folder and Save

To open the attachment:

1 Click the Windows button and choose Documents or Pictures as appropriate

2 Double-click the file. It will open in the relevant application

Beware

You can open the attachment by opening the email message and double-clicking on the attachment name. However, this is a temporary copy and should not be used to make changes.

Hot tip

Sometimes, if you receive a formatted email as plain text, the formatted version will be shown as an attachment of type .htm. See page 75 for email options.

77

Contacts

Your Contacts list acts as your address book and can be used to contain a wide range of details about family, friends and businesses. Details such as work address, birthdays and anniversaries, as well as the usual home address, email and phone numbers can be stored. You can even add a photograph.

To create a contact:

1 Open Windows Mail and select Tools, Windows Contacts or click the Contacts button on the toolbar

2 Click New Contact to open the Properties window and complete your contact's details

3 Use the Tab key to move between fields. The Full Name field will be completed automatically. Click the down arrow to choose the display attributes

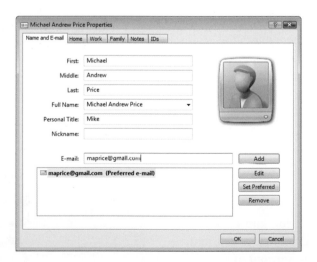

4 Complete the email address and click Add. The address will be moved to the email box and the text Preferred e-mail added. If your contact has more than one email address, you can select which to use

Other methods of adding contacts to your Contacts folder include:

1 Right-click the message header in your Inbox and click Add Sender to Contacts

2 Open the message and right-click the sender's email address. Then choose Add to Contacts

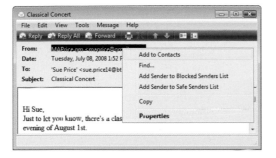

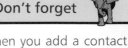
Don't forget

When you add a contact using any of these methods, only the email address field will be completed.

3 Open Tools, Options and click the Send Tab. Tick the option to Automatically put people I reply to in my Contacts list (see page 75)

Use the Contacts list to create email

1 With the Contacts list open, click the contact's name and then single click the contact's email address in the right hand pane. This will open Windows Mail with the address bar completed

2 As a useful alternative, customise the Side Bar on the desktop to display your Contacts list. Then simply scroll to the required name and click the email address

Hot tip

To edit or amend your contact's details, open the Contacts list and double-click the contact's name.

Hot tip

The Contacts list in the Side Bar also displays the contact's telephone number if completed.

Note: the Contacts list in the Side Bar is only updated with amendments when the PC is restarted.

79

Contact Group

Creating a group of contacts makes it easier to communicate with a selection of your contacts. You send the email to all the contacts in the group in one easy step, without having to address them individually. To create a Contact Group:

1 Open the Contacts window and click the New Contact Group button

2 Supply a group name and then click Add to Contact Group

3 Select the names from your Contacts holding down the Ctrl key as you click. This enables you to choose several individual names at one time

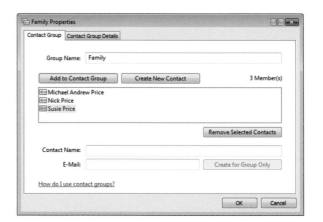

4 If you have email contacts that you only want to appear in the Group and not in your main Contacts list, use the facility to add a Contact Name and E-mail address and Create for Group only

5 Click OK when finished and you will see the Group listed in alphabetical order in the Contacts window

Manage Your Email

Windows Mail is structured with a series of folders to contain and organize your mail.

- Inbox is where your mail arrives and is usually stored

- Outbox holds the messages you create until you initiate Send and Receive

- Sent items contains a copy of all messages sent

- Deleted items stores messages that you no longer want

- Drafts contains email messages that you wish to complete and send later

- Junk mail holds items that either you or Windows Mail considers to be unwanted or unsolicited messages

You can create your own folders to organize your mail:

1 Right-click the Inbox and select New Folder

2 Name the folder and select the folder to contain the subfolder. Then click OK

3 Drag and drop mail from the Inbox to the new folder, or to any other folder, for example Deleted Items

4 To sort items within any folder, click a label (From, Subject or Received) on the header bar

Hot tip

Junk mail may be called Bulk mail in web-based email.

Hot tip

A second click on the Header bar will reverse the order.

Junk Email

Junk email, or spam, is the computerised equivalent of the unsolicited mail that comes through your door every day. Most ISPs provide filters that will try to eliminate or redirect spam so that it doesn't actually reach your computer. Your antivirus program may redirect suspect mail. Windows Mail lets you set up your own rules to redirect any junk mail that may get through.

1 Click Tools on the Windows Mail toolbar and choose Junk E-mail Options

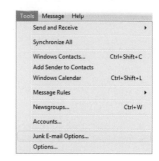

2 View the option selected and decide if it meets your requirements

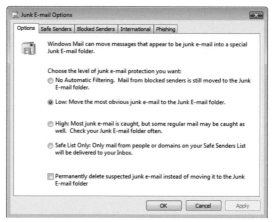

3 Click the Safe Senders and Blocked Senders tabs in turn and add any specific email addresses or domain names

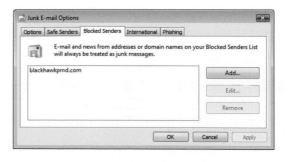

You should check your Junk mail folder at regular intervals to ensure that messages are correctly diverted. To reclassify your messages:

1 Right-click the message and select Junk e-mail

Use Tools, Message rules, in Windows Mail, to set specific actions to be taken when messages arrive. You could, for example, move email from certain contacts or that contains specific words in the Subject, directly into a projects folder.

2 If the message has already been transferred to the Junk Mail folder, you will also have the option to Mark as not junk

If you use PC based mail, you should also from time to time, check to see if any valid or expected email have been trapped by your ISP. For example:

1 Connect to the Internet and sign on to your email account

2 Click and view the Bulk or Spam folder. The message in the Bulk folder is, in this instance, not spam

3 Select the message and move it to the Inbox. Sign out of the online mail. When you start Windows Mail, it will be downloaded at the next Send/Receive

Email Hints and Tips

1 You may receive email messages from banks and other organizations with which you conduct business. The message will usually contain information about your account and inform you that you cannot use this address for correspondence, for example:
NoReply-FlyingBlue@airfrance.fr
These messages are automatically generated and are not monitored email addresses

2 Occasionally, an email will fail to arrive. There are several causes. It may be that you typed an incorrect email address, or the contact's server was off-line or busy. In these cases you will usually receive an error message.

Check the email address and if that is correct, just try again later, when the server may be back in service

3 With important messages, you can add a priority flag to attract the attention of the recipient. More effectively, you can add a Read Receipt to the message. When the recipient opens the message, you will be notified. Select Tools, Request Read Receipt

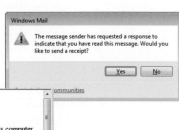

4 For security reasons, many email messages that you receive will have their pictures blocked. You should decide if you recognize or trust the site before you proceed to download the images

5 You can unsubscribe to websites when you no longer wish to receive newsletters or updates from them. The site will usually indicate how to do this. However, with unsolicited email messages, avoid unsubscribing as this will actually validate your email address with the spammer

85

6 Many websites include the option to send an email with a link to a specific page. However, you can email the web page address separately:
Click in the address bar, the address will be highlighted
Press Ctrl+C to copy
Open your email program
Click in the message area of the email
Press Ctrl+V to insert or paste

Newsgroups

A newsgroup is a discussion group on the Internet, open to all and centred around a mutual interest or topic. Newsgroups can be a valuable source of help and information on topics as wide ranging as Archeology to Zoology, Terry Pratchett to rocket maintenance. The newsgroup community is important to many participants, it means they can discuss their interest with those of a like mind.

Newsgroups evolved from basic text bulletin boards where scientists and students placed information about their interests and hobbies. With the introduction of the more sophisticated HTTP (HyperText Transfer Protocol), movies, pictures and music files can be shared.

To be able to participate in a newsgroup, you need to use a program such as Windows Mail or Netscape Communicator. When you subscribe to the newsgroup, you can post messages and participate in 'conversations'. You can see answers to questions and follow threads. You use your email program to do this, when you post a comment or reply, everyone can see the message.

Microsoft Communities is a collection of newgroups relating to Microsoft Windows and Office software that has already been set up in Windows Mail.

1 Click Microsoft Communities in the Folder pane and choose to view the list of available newsgroups

2 With the list of topics displayed, type your area of interest in the Display newsgroups bar and the list will scroll to that point. Note that the newsgroups cover a variety of languages and countries. The .fr., .it., .jp., in the newsgroup name refers to the language

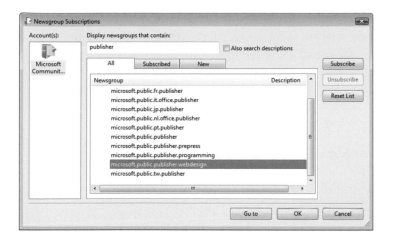

3 Click the Goto button to view the newsgroup and click the + next to an item to expand the conversation

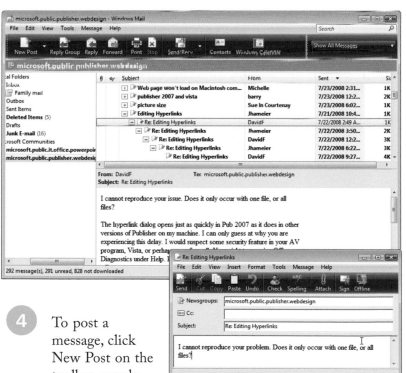

4 To post a message, click New Post on the toolbar, supply your name and the email address to use and create your message. Click Send when finished

Hot tip

Newsgroup Netiquette is basic etiquette for posting messages and replies. Many sites will give you guidelines for best practice. Good sites are well monitored and moderated.

Hot tip

When you leave the newsgroup, you will be asked if you wish to subscribe. Right-click the newsgroup in the folder list and choose Unsubscribe if you wish to no longer receive postings.

Other Newsgroup Servers

You may wish to subscribe to other newsgroups. Your ISP will provide a newsgroup server, that gives you access to the wide range of general topics. To add this server to Windows Mail:

1 Click Tools, Accounts and Add. Select Newsgroup Account from the following window and then Next

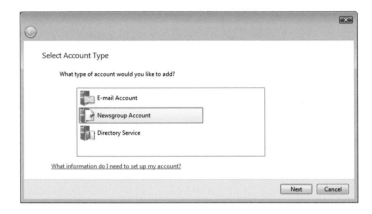

2 Supply your preferred name and click Next, the email address to use and again click Next

3 Type the name of the server as supplied by your ISP, click Next and Finish

Hot tip

Where your news server requires you to log on, and has given you an account name and password, this is usually a paid service.

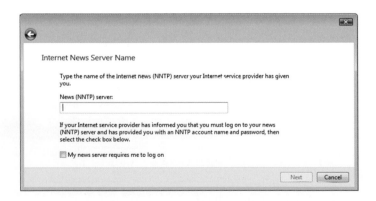

4 You will see the new Newsgroup server listed in the folder pane. To access the individual newsgroups, follow the same procedure as for Microsoft Communities

Instant Messaging

If you have a full DSL (broadband) connection, you can use your computer to communicate live with others. This may take the form of typing messages or by voice, and with a camera attached, you can send live video.

There are lots of software programs that enable live communication, one of the most popular is Skype. This is available as a free download from **www.skype.com.**

1 Visit the Skype website and click the Download Now button

2 Follow the on-screen instructions to run the file. Skype will be downloaded to a temporary folder on your computer

3 Accept the terms and conditions and click Install

4 You will need to close any open programs as recommended by Skype and reboot the computer

5 When you start Skype for the first time you will have to sign in and choose a Skype name and set a log in id and password

Hot tip

Skype also lets you make cheap calls to phones and mobile phones all over the world.

Don't forget

Skype is available for most versions of Windows operating systems. The main Skype window lists hardware requirements for Skype to run.

Hot tip

Use the Getting Started tutorial to discover how to check that your sound works, to add contacts and start calling your friends.

...cont'd

6 Add contacts either by selecting Add Contact or by using Search for Users. With either method, Skype will search for and list matching names to help you locate the correct person. Select Tools, Import, to get Skype to search your Address Book for those who are already using Skype

7 To start a conversation, double-click the contact's name, or if their name is already selected, just click on the green telephone

8 With a microphone attached, you can have a normal conversation, otherwise you will need to type. With a camera attached, click Start My Video to enable your contact to see you

9 Use Tools, Options and select Video Settings to manage your camera and other associated options

6 Surfing the Internet

The Internet is an enormous resource, so you need to find your way around using web addresses and using search engines to locate websites and web pages of interest. Internet Explorer helps, with tabbed browsing and with favorites and history. You can choose a home page, save pages of interest and print web pages. As you get used to the Internet, you can move on to cost effective shopping, investing and banking online.

What's Needed

The requirements for accessing websites on the Internet are similar to those for electronic mail communications (see page 70):

- Computer with Internet connection
- Account with an Internet Service Provider (ISP)

In addition, you will require:

- Internet browser software such as Internet Explorer
- Antivirus software and other security add-ins

To start Internet Explorer:

1 Select Start and then click the browser link (in this case Internet Explorer) at the top of the Start menu

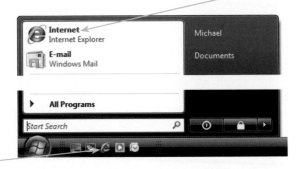

2 The browser will open and display the default startup web page, in this example **http://www.nba.com**

Don't forget

Internet Explorer is the Internet browser provided with Windows Vista. Other Internet browsers include Mozilla, Firefox and Opera.

Hot tip

Alternatively, click the browser icon that's shown on the Quick Launch bar.

Hot tip

The default startup web page is known as your Home Page. You can choose any web page you wish to act as your home page.

3 To view a web page, click in the address bar area, type the address e.g. **www.nationalgeographic.com** and press Enter

Hot tip

When you click in the address bar, the current address is highlighted. Click a second time to amend the address, or just start to type and the whole address is replaced.

4 The requested web page is displayed. Click one of the links to switch to a related web page, for example **Maps** which displays **www.nationalgeographic.com/maps**

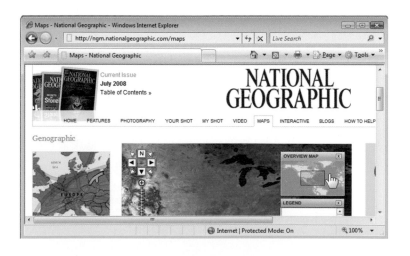

Don't forget

Text links to other web pages are often underlined. Sometimes the underlining will only appear when you move the mouse over the selectable area.

Hot tip

Images and graphics can also have associated web page links. You can always identify a link (picture or text), since the mouse pointer changes to a hand symbol.

Web Addresses

The full web page address for National Geographic maps is:

http://nga.nationalgeographic.com/maps/index.html

This address is also known as a URL (universal resource locator) and it contains the following parts:

http://	Hypertext Transfer Protocol (protocol used for transferring web pages)
nga.nationalgeographic.com	host name of computer
maps	Directory structure (one or more folders)
index.html	File name of web page

The host name of the computer ends with an extension that usually indicates the type of institution. The values can include:

.com commercial institution

.net commercial institution (addition to .com)

.edu educational institution

.org not-for-profit organization

.gov government institution

.mil military

The extension may also indicate the country where the institution is located, for example:

.at	Austria
.au	Australia
.ca	Canada
.uk	United Kingdom

If no web page name is provided, the browser will look for a default name, trying a variety of names including:

default.htm	default.asp	index.php
index.html	index.htm	index.shtml

Search for Web Pages

If you aren't sure of the exact web page address, or just interested to find useful pages, you can use the Instant Search Box.

1 Click in the search box, type a relevant word or phrase, for example **Night sky**, and then press Enter

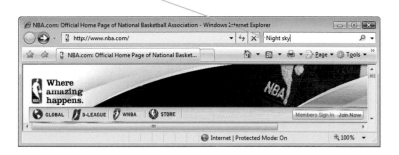

2 Links to the first ten web pages are listed, along with the total number of matches – in this case over 62 million

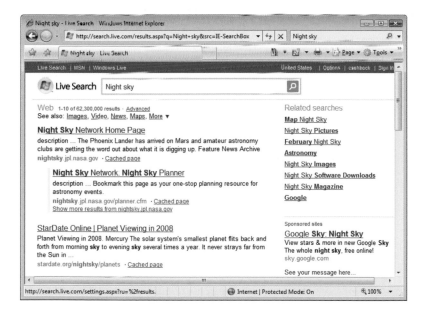

3 Select a suitable web page, or scroll down and select another set of ten matches

Hot tip

By default, Internet Explorer uses Microsoft's Live Search, but you can change the search provider (see page 96).

Don't forget

You can switch to lists of Images, Video, News, Maps or other items, all based on the same search text as the web page list.

Hot tip

You may be offered a list of related searches, and there may be several Sponsored Sites that have paid a fee to be positioned prominently on the results page.

Change Search Provider

You can have different search providers in addition to or in place of the Microsoft Live Search default.

1 Click the arrow at the right of the Instant Search Box and choose Find More Providers

Don't forget

You can add a provider as an alternative for occasional use or as the new default option.

Hot tip

The selected provider becomes the temporary default until you end the session or you select a different provider.

Don't forget

Click Change Search Defaults to remove an entry or to amend the default permanently.

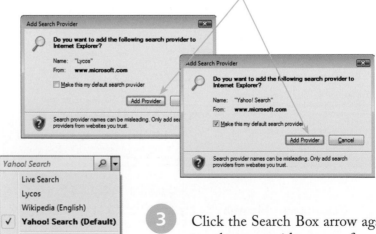

2 Select a search provider, click Make this my default search provider if desired, then click Add Provider

3 Click the Search Box arrow again to select a provider to use for the remainder of the Internet Explorer session

Page Back and Forward

When you view new web pages, your browser remembers the pages that you have already visited.

1 Click the back arrow to go back to the previous page

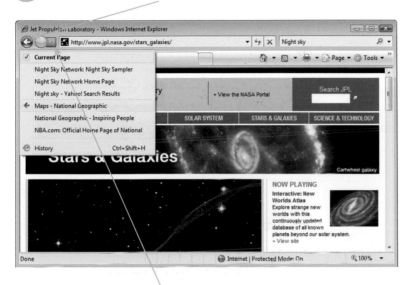

Hot tip

Click the Back icon to display the immediately previous page.

2 Click the down arrow to list all the pages you've viewed, and click any entry to switch to that place in the sequence

Don't forget

When you view a previous page, the Forward icon is enabled and will display the next page in the sequence.

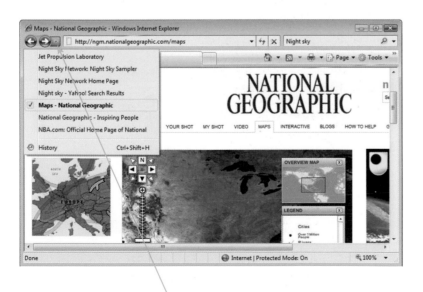

Beware

If you select any link on one of the previous pages, the record from that point on will be discarded and replaced by the newly selected page, unless you use a new window or new tab (see page 98).

3 Click the down arrow again to select a different page

Open New Window

You can open a new browser window, to avoid discarding an existing sequence of pages. The options include:

1 Select the Internet Explorer icon from the Start menu or Launch bar to open a separate copy at the Home page

2 Right-click the required link and select Open in New Window to display that web page

3 Press Ctrl+N to open the current web page in a new window, then select the required link

Use Tabbed Browsing

With Internet Explorer 7.0 and later versions you have the option to use tabs to display multiple web pages in the same window.

1   Type a web page address and press Alt+Enter to open the page on a separate tab and make it the foreground tab

2   Right-click a hyperlink and select Open in New Tab

3   Type keywords in the search box and press Alt+Enter to carry out the search on a new tab

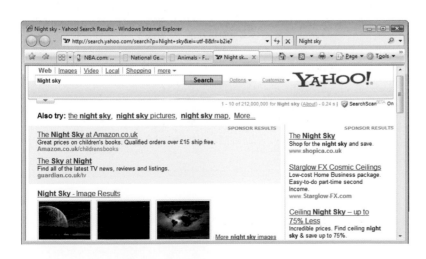

Don't forget

To open a new blank tab, click the New Tab button (or press Ctrl+T).

Hot tip

You can also press Ctrl then left-click the link. In either case, the current tab remains in the foreground. Press Ctrl+Shift and click the link to make it become the foreground.

Don't forget

Click any tab to switch to that tab as foreground, or press Ctrl+n where n is tab number 1-8. Ctrl+9 selects the last tab, however many tabs there are.

Quick Tabs

When you have more than one tab in use, the Quick Tabs button appears to the left of the row of tabs.

Don't forget

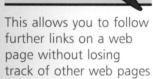

As more tabs are opened, the web page titles are truncated and eventually scroll buttons will be added.

1 Click the down arrow next to the Quick Tabs button to display the full names of the web pages on the tabs

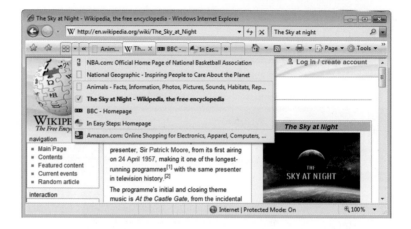

Hot tip

This allows you to follow further links on a web page without losing track of other web pages that you have visited.

2 Click any web page title to make that tab the foreground

3 Click the Quick Tabs button itself to display miniature thumbnails of the pages, to help select the required one

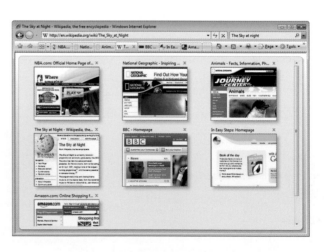

Hot tip

Click the Quick Tabs button again to switch off Quick Tabs view and return to the previously viewed tab.

4 Click a web page thumbnail to view it, or click the ⊠ at the top right of the thumbnail to close that tab

...cont'd

1 To close a tab from the tab row, click the tab to bring it to the foreground, then click the **X** that appears

2 To close all the tabs, click the on the main window

3 Select Close Tabs or select Show Options to choose to open the same set of tabs next time you start the browser

Don't forget

With only one tab in effect, clicking the Close button ends Internet Explorer without any interaction.

101

Hot tip

Click the Cancel button if you change your mind about closing the tabs.

Don't forget

The set of tabs are remembered for the next time only. On future restarts, just the home page will open.

View Details

Web pages can be filled with lots of information, and sometimes use small text sizes to fit everything onto the page. There are several ways to make things easier to see:

1 Click Page then click Text Size, where Medium is the default, and choose your preferred size

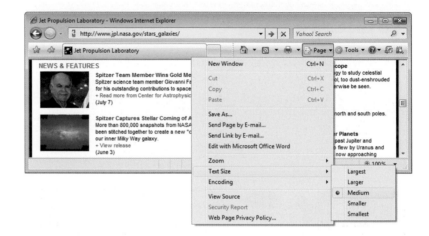

2 To enlarge the graphics, and images as well as text, click the arrow next to the Zoom button and select the scale

3 Select Custom to specify an exact scale 10% - 1000%. The small scale factors are useful for overviews of web pages

Internet Explorer has particular support for large images.

1 Click on the image of the Taj Mahal at Wikipedia

2 What's displayed is a small image that shows the whole of the picture. Note the Magnify cursor

3 Click on the image to expand it

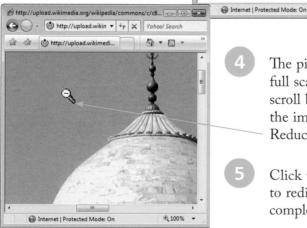

4 The picture is shown full scale. Use the scroll bars to explore the image. Note the Reduce cursor

5 Click the image to redisplay the complete image

Web Address Reminder

When you want to repeat a web address that you've visited previously, Internet Explorer can remind you of the full address.

Don't forget

The addresses are shown in the sequence they were typed, with the newest addresses at the top. Use the scroll bar to view more addresses.

1 Click the down arrow at the end of the address bar and select an address from those you've typed previously

2 Type the first part of the address, and select the full web page address when it appears

Hot tip

Matching alternatives appear as you type. The one you want appears when you've typed enough to identify it.

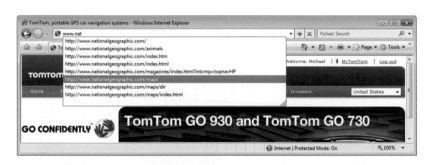

You can also use the Instant Search box (see page 42) or carry out a search from the Address bar.

3 Type appropriate keywords or page name and press Enter, or press Alt+Enter to display the results on a new tab

Hot tip

For clarity, you can prefix the search text with the command Find, Go or ? when you enter a search on the address bar.

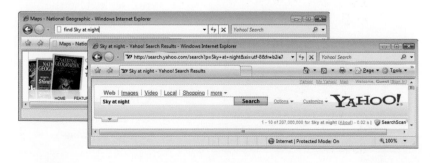

Favorites Center

Internet Explorer keeps a note of all the websites and web pages you visit. To review your browsing history:

1 Click the Favorites Center button and select the View History button

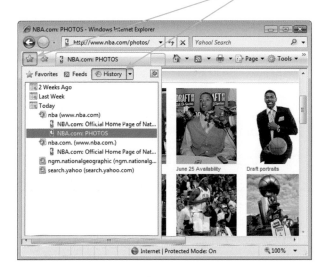

Don't forget

The Favorites Center includes web page Favorites (see page 106), RSS Feeds (see page 132) and the browsing History, as discussed on this page.

2 Type a day or week to expand the contents. Click a website entry to show the web pages viewed

3 Select a web page to view its contents. This removes the History list from view

Hot tip

To keep the list you'd click which turns to an ✕ and the Favorites Center will be pinned to the window.

4 To change the sequence in which the History is displayed, click the arrow next to the View History button and choose By Date, By Site, By Most Visited, or By Order Visited Today

5 Choose Search History and type keywords, then click Search Now to list the web pages that have those words included in their titles

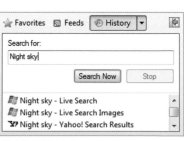

When you find a web page that you know you'll want to visit again, you can add it to your Favorites list.

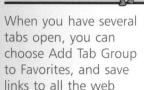

1 While viewing the web page, click the Add to Favorites button, and then click Add to Favorites

2 Accept the suggested name or type a new name

3 If required, click the down arrow to choose a different folder

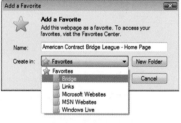

4 Click Add to place the web page reference in the specified folder

5 Click Favorites Center and then select Favorites

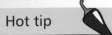

Home Pages

If there's a page you'd always want to start off with, you can make it your home page or add it to your set of home page tabs.

1 Visit the web page, for example **www.google.com**

Don't forget

When you change your home page or home page tabs, you can save the results as a Favorite web page or Favorite tab group, so you can easily restore your home page settings in the future.

2 Click the arrow next to the Home button and select Add or Change Home Page

3 Choose the appropriate option

Beware

The option to use the current tab set as your home page will be offered only if you have more than one tab open in Internet Explorer.

4 Click Yes to save your changes

Save Web Page

Another way to make sure that you can always access the contents of a particular web page is to save it on your hard disk.

If you save the web page to disk, you'll be able to review the contents even when you are not online to the Internet.

1 With the web page displayed, click the Page button and select the Save As entry from the list

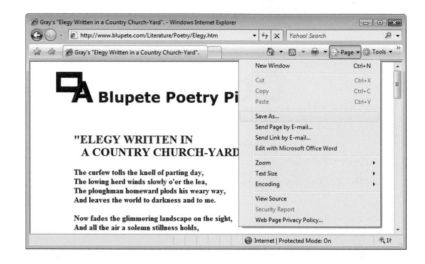

Hot tip

You can save all the content of the web page including graphics and frames, or save the text content only in .html or .txt format.

```
Webpage, complete (*.htm;*.html)
Web Archive, single file (*.mht)
Webpage, HTML only (*.htm;*.html)
Text File (*.txt)
```

2 Change the suggested file name if desired then click the arrow on Save As Type and select the type, e.g. .txt

Hot tip

Click Browse Folder to select a different location for the file. You can view the .txt file in Notepad. Use Internet Explorer for the other file types.

3 Click the Save button to save the file onto the hard disk

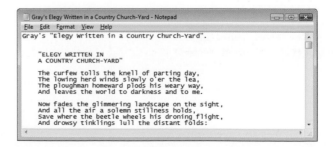

You can let others know about web pages you find interesting.

1 Open the web page in Internet Explorer and click Page

Hot tip

Internet Explorer will create a message form using your default email program, in this case Windows Mail.

2 Select Send Page by Email to send the actual content of the web page in an email message

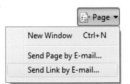

Beware

The layout of the web page may be different in the email message. For that reason, it is usually better to send the address rather than the actual page.

3 Select Send Link by Email to send the web page address (URL) in the email message

Don't forget

You must add email addresses for all the recipients, a suitable title and any accompanying text message needed.

Print Web Page

1 To see how the current web page will print, click the arrow next to the Print button and select Print Preview

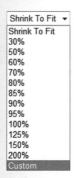

2 By default, Internet Explorer will shrink the page to fit the paper, in this case using a scale value of 85%

3 Click the Print Document button to send the web page to the printer, or press Esc to end the print preview

Shopping on the Internet

1 To see a typical shopping website, visit **www.amazon.com**

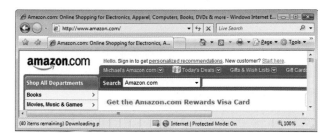

Don't forget

One of the great benefits of the Internet is with shopping. You can use websites to help you identify the best products and where to find them. Often, you'll get the best prices by completing the purchase at a website.

2 Click Start Here, enter your email ID and click Sign In

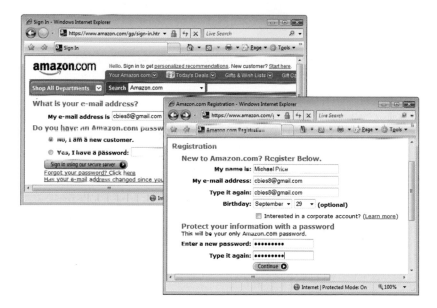

Beware

If you visit Amazon. com from a region other than the USA, you'll be advised to switch to the local Amazon website.

3 Now you can explore and search the website for books etc.

Hot tip

All that's needed to register at the Amazon website is your email address, name, date of birth and a password.

Hot tip

Choose a department such as Books or Cameras or Computers, and browse the products or type a search keyword to find specific items.

...cont'd

Don't forget

Click Your Account and select Your Browsing History Settings, to find the button to Turn Off Browsing History, if you'd rather not have this information stored.

Hot tip

Amazon suggests related items that might be of interest. You are also encouraged to buy more to qualify your order for free shipping.

Beware

Treat the 1-Click option with caution, since orders may be placed without a confirmation step. Fortunately this featured is turned off by default.

4 Amazon remembers the products you review, and will make recommendations based on your browsing history

5 When you've found something you want, click Add to Cart. A summary of your shopping cart is displayed

6 Click Edit Shopping Cart to change the quantities or remove items

To display and edit the contents of the shopping cart at any time, click the View Cart icon at the top of the page.

Place Your Order

1 Click the Proceed to Checkout button, and sign in with email ID and password

2 Enter the shipping address, choose a shipping option then select the payment method that suits you

3 Review your order and click Place Your Order to confirm

Don't forget

Adding an item to your shopping cart doesn't reserve the item, and there's no commitment to purchase until you actually place your order.

Beware

If you register at the USA site but are located overseas, your orders will be sent by international shipping. It's much better to register and place orders at your local Amazon website.

Hot tip

Amazon offers a variety of payment methods, including credit card, store card, checking account, money order and an option to be billed for the order.

Don't forget

The progress bar shows the steps for preparing and submitting your order. The final step commits you to the purchase.

Money Management

1 Visit **finance.yahoo.com** and click a tab such as Investing

2 You can participate in online banking which will give you 24/7 access to your checking and savings accounts

3 The address bar background shows the security status: Red – out of date or invalid, Yellow – unverified, White – normal validation, Green – extended validation

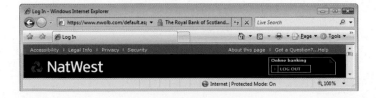

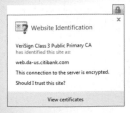

7 Personal Internet

Make the Internet personal for you. You can create and manage your own website, starting with a free service then moving on to your own domain. Set up a blog or web diary on your website, or on a specialized service. Participate in a social network or take advantage of web feeds. You can even use the Internet to explore your own family tree.

Create a Website

Hot tip

Many ISPs offer storage space on their Internet servers for you to create your own website, or you can use a dedicated website host, free or fee based.

Don't forget

Start off with a free website host, or one that offers a free trial. If you decide to continue, you can switch to a more permanent setup.

Don't forget

Freewebs.com checks that the user name you specify is still available, advising you to try another if the one you want has already been allocated.

Username is unavailable.
Try another one.

Perhaps the best way to understand the Internet is to create your own website. It isn't as difficult as you might think, and it needn't be expensive. In fact we can start off with a completely free website, just to get a feel for what might be involved and whether it might be something worth pursuing more seriously.

You'll need a name for your website, an associated email address, somewhere to store your web pages (the website host) and facilities for creating and updating web pages. For our example website, we'll use one of the free website host services.

1 Visit the website **www.freewebs.com** and click Start Now

2 Specify your desired Freewebs user name, which will also be used as your website address

3 Provide the other details requested - password, site title, email address, year of birth, country and gender

④ Scroll down to the next section and select a template and color for your site, for example the Clipboard in Blue

Don't forget

If you already have a site to upload to and don't want to use the FreeWebs Site Builder tools, click to Use Advanced (HTML) Mode.

⑤ Check the box to agree to the terms of service and click Create My Site

⑥ Select the website package you want (either No Ads or Enhanced) or click Continue for the basic, free package

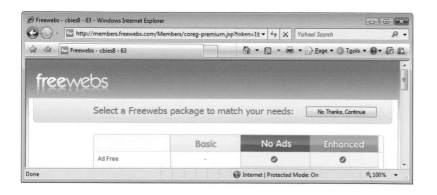

Hot tip

The alternative packages provide extra features and support, plus they avoid the banner ads (see page 123) that cover the cost of the facilities.

Choose Website Type

1 Select Help me build my site if you want a starter setup

2 Specify the main classification of your website - personal, professional & small business or clubs & groups

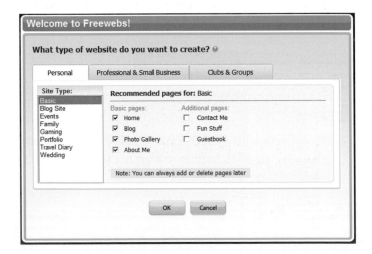

3 Select the specific type from the list offered, then decide which particular pages you want to include at this time

4 Click OK to create sample pages for each of these

If you prefer you can build your website from a blank sheet, adding pages and components as you wish.

1 Select Start building on my own

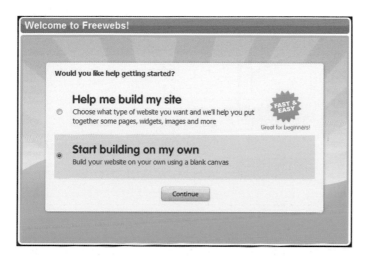

2 You'll be given a blank home page to start off with. Click the Content Box button to start creating the web page

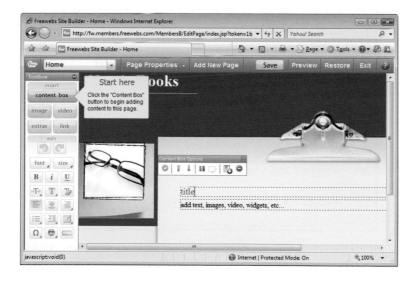

3 Provide the title for the section and add the text, image, video, link or application content required

Don't forget

The page will use your chosen template. However, you can change templates at any time, and the change is applied to all the web pages you've created.

Hot tip

The first web page will be automatically labeled as the Home page and given the file name index.htm.

Add an Image

1 Click in the content area and select the image button

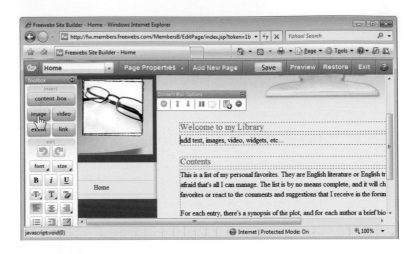

2 Choose the image you want to insert, or click Upload New Image to add a new image from your computer

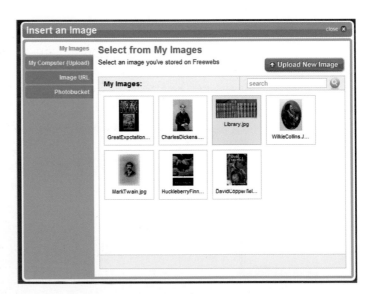

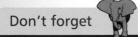
3 When the image is inserted, the Image Options toolbar is displayed, allowing you to edit, align, frame, resize or delete

Add a Page

1 Click the Add New Page button to select the type of page required

Hot tip

You can add all the pages needed and build their content later, or create each page as you go along.

2 Add an empty page or choose a page setup ready for use as a photo album, blog, guest book etc., using the current template for styles and layout

3 Click the Save button, then click Save Draft to save all the changes to the current page

Don't forget

You can also choose to publish the changes to the Internet so that they are immediately available to anyone who views your website.

4 Click the Exit button and click Save as draft and exit to save all changes to your web pages

Hot tip

If you've completed all your changes, click the box to Publish all pages, and click Publish Changes to make the new pages available on the Internet.

Site Management

1 The Site Manager lists all the pages in your website

2 Click an order button to sequence entries on the Navbar

3 Select Edit Titles & Footers to make changes to the website title or to add a website slogan or tagline

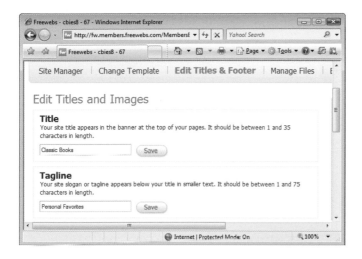

Don't forget

Click the Save button to apply the changes to your website details.

4 Select the See My Site button at the top of the page to begin exploring your website

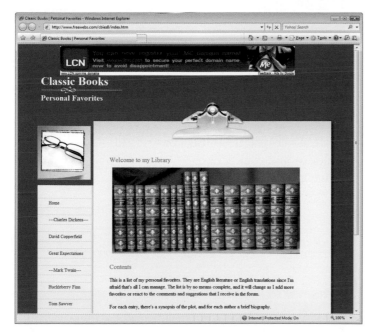

Hot tip

Note the advertising banner added to the top of your web pages. This will be removed if you opt for a premium rather than a free website.

Don't forget

Click the entries on the Navbar to view other web pages in your website.

Website Addresses

To view and change the address used to access your website:

1 Logon to the Freewebs site with your user name and password

2 Select My Account link for the user name

3 Review the account info, in particular the Primary Web Address

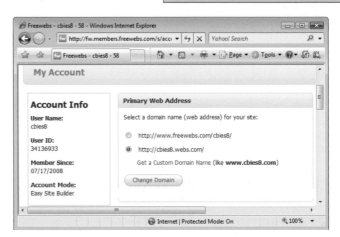

4 Select your preferred form of website address and click Change Domain then click See My Site

The default is www.freewebs.com/username but you can switch to the professional looking username.webs.com. However, for the most authentic address, you need to obtain a domain name, giving you a website address such as www.username.com.

124

Don't forget

This is the website address that you'd give to friends and family so that they can visit your website.

Hot tip

Note how the Google Adsense ads are selected according to the context of your web page.

Blogging

A blog (short for web log) is a website with regular journal style entries such as event descriptions or comments. The entries are usually text but they may include pictures, videos and links to other blogs or web pages. Blogs can be personal or corporate, and may be individual websites or hosted on a specialised server. To create a website blog using Freewebs.com:

1 Register a website name and title at Freewebs.com, choose Personal and Blog Site and click OK

Hot tip

The suggested website contains a Home page, a Blog page for entries and an About page. Also offered are Photo Gallery, Profile and Guestbook web pages.

2 Follow the Sitewizard prompts to create the Home page

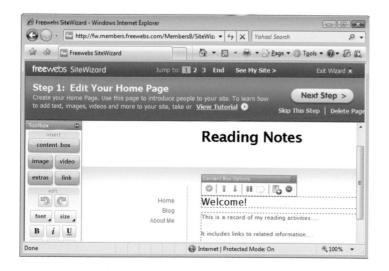

Don't forget

The home page sets the context for the blog and provides any background information considered necessary.

Add a Blog Entry

Hot tip

You provide a title and the content for the entry, and formatting is automatically applied. You can change the text formatting using the toolbar. You can also insert hyperlinks, lines, tables, images, videos and audio clips.

Hot tip

The privacy options allow you to make particular entries available to everyone, to other Freewebs users only, or to yourself alone.

Don't forget

For future entries, log in to Freewebs, edit the Blog page and click the Post New Entry button.

1 The Sitewizard helps you complete the first blog entry

2 The final page usually provides details of the blog author

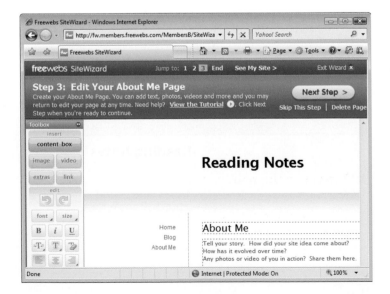

View Blog

1 Your friends can view your website on the Internet, using the appropriate form of website address

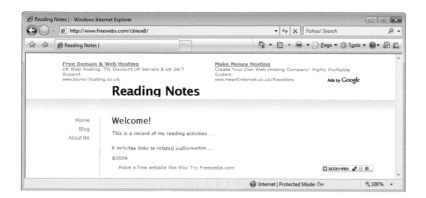

Hot tip

If your website is free, Adsense ads will be added as a banner at the top of the page.

2 Click the Blog link to display the entries, with the latest at the top of the list if there's more than one

Hot tip

The template contains a Navbar area that will list all the names of the web pages as they are added. The position depends on the particular template.

3 Visitors to the website can post comments and view the comments already posted, so an interesting entry can develop into a conversation in its own right

Don't forget

Visitors can right-click the Permalink and then select Add to Favorites, to get a direct link to that particular entry for future visits, perhaps to check up on comments.

Blogging Service

1 Visit **www.blogger.com,** specify your Google email
address (or create a Google account) and click Sign In

2 Specify your display name and continue as directed

3 Type the title and the name to use for your blog

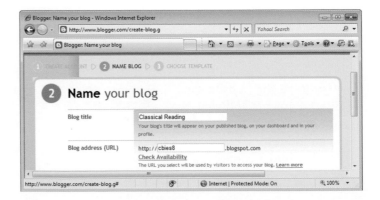

4 Select a template to apply to your blog. Your selection can be changed later if you wish

5 When the blog has been created, you can create the first entry and click Publish Post to make it ready for viewing

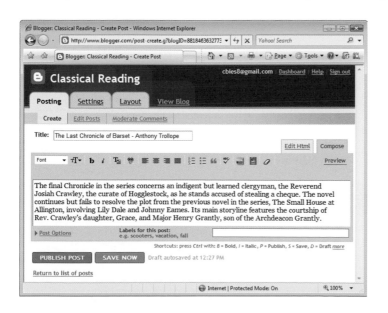

Hot tip

There are relatively few templates, about 40 color variations included. However, you can add various page elements and you can edit the underlying HTML code, to customize your blog.

Hot tip

As with the Freewebs blog, you can format the text and add images, videos and other items to your entries.

Don't forget

To add posts in future, sign in to Blogger.com and click New Post for the required blog.

Manage Your Blogs   Create a Blog | Help

Classical Reading   View Blog
1 Post, last published on Jul 23, 2008

New Post   Manage: Posts, Settings, Layout

Social Networking

You can use the Internet to help keep in touch with friends and others with shared interests. Popular sites include MySpace, YouTube and Facebook. Originally the preserve of the 18 to 24 age group, these sites have been opened up for anyone to join, businesses and political parties included.

For example, you can use Facebook to join a regional network and connect with the people in your area.

1 Go to **www.facebook.com** and provide the personal details requested, then click the Sign Up button

2 Copy the text displayed. This is a security check to prevent automated responders creating accounts

3 You'll be asked to confirm your email address by responding to the email message that Facebook sends to you

130

4   Locate the email from Facebook and select the hyperlink

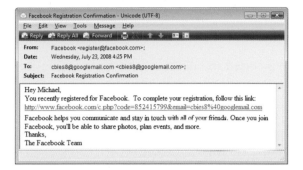

You can allow Facebook to use your address book and locate contacts that may already be registered, or click Skip to take things more slowly, until you get used to the system.

5   Complete the registration with as much detail as you wish

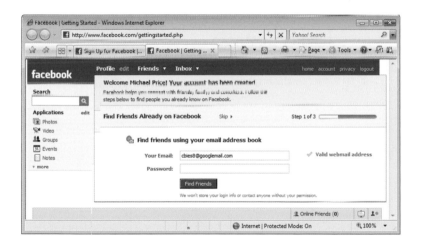

Don't forget

Facebook is made up of many networks, based around companies, regions or schools. Join the networks that reflect your personal circumstances to learn about people who work, live or study near you.

6   Invite friends individually to join you on Facebook

Beware

Avoid revealing personal information on social networking sites. You never know who might be visiting your account.

RSS Web Feeds

Hot tip

RSS stands for Really Simple Syndication and it is a mechanism for distributing lists of headlines, update notices and additions.

If you are interested in any regularly changing website, you may be able to keep up to date with the changes without having to actually visit the site. Most such sites now offer an RSS web feed. It avoids you having to log on to the sites, just in case there are some changes, or subscribing to different newsletters for each site.

Originally supported through special software, support for RSS is now built in to your browser. This lets you know when RSS web feeds are available, and helps you view and subscribe to them.

1 When you visit a website, Internet Explorer automatically searches for RSS web feeds

2 The greyed RSS icon indicates that no feeds were located on the browser toolbar

Beware

Some websites use an icon such as RSS on the web page to indicate that feeds are available. For an example, see www.reuters.com.

Do More With Reuters

‣ RSS
‣ Mobile
‣ Podcasts
‣ Newsletters
‣ You Witness News

3 When the RSS icon changes color and (optionally) a sound is played, you know that feeds have been detected

4 Click the RSS icon to list the feeds on that web page

5 Click the RSS icon, and select an RSS feed name to view the current news items for that feed

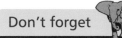
Don't forget

Options are provided to sequence the news items, by date or alphabetically by title.

6 Click Subscribe to this Feed, then click the Subscribe button, to add it to the list of feeds managed by your browser

Hot tip

As with Favorites, you can select or create a folder, to help organize your list of feeds.

7 Click the Favorites Center button then click the Feeds button, to view the feeds being monitored

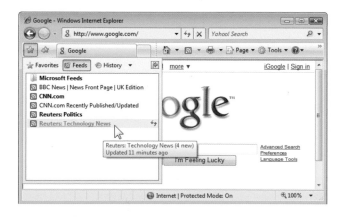

Don't forget

Highlighted entries indicate those with new entries for viewing. Move the mouse over an entry to see a summary of the feed contents.

Settings for Feeds

To change settings for your RSS feeds

1 Click Tools, select Internet Options, then click Content tab

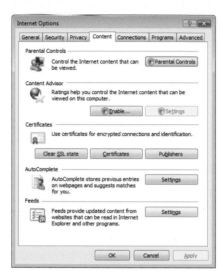

2 Locate the Feeds section and click the Settings button

Don't forget

Have your feeds updated as often as once every 15 minutes, or leave as much as a week between updates.

15 minutes
30 minutes
1 hour
4 hours
1 day
1 week

3 Choose to automatically check feeds for updates and set the frequency

4 The Advanced settings control the way feeds are displayed and also allow you to specify an audio signal when feeds are detected on a web page

Hot tip

Some feeds provide a Properties link where you can make adjustments such as the number of recent items to be retained.

Genealogy on the Internet

The Internet can also be the place to locate personal information. If you are new to Genealogy, there are numerous tutorials online to help you get started. For example:

 1   ProQuest   **www.proquest.com/product_hq/gen101/**

This is an introductory tutorial that outlines the practical and online stages involved in building your own family's history.

Other Genealogy websites that may help you locate the information you need include:

 1   Cyndi's List   **www.cyndislist.com/**

Cyndi's List provides a categorized and cross-referenced index to reliable and trustworthy genealogical research websites and resources on the Internet.

135

Hot tip

There are literally thousands of websites and databases available on the Internet with the records and information you need to help you trace your family tree.

Hot tip

This tutorial helps you understand that the Internet and online sources follow on from conventional research techniques.

Don't forget

Cyndi's List can act as an excellent starting point for your online research.

...cont'd

2   FamilySearch   **www.familysearch.org**

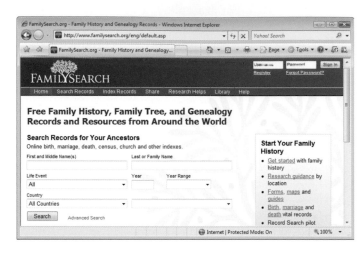

Hot tip

This website also offers access to transcriptions of the 1880 U.S. Census and the 1881 British and Canadian Census.

At the FamilySearch website you can view many records from the extensive family history library maintained by The Church of Jesus Christ of Latter-day Saints

3   Genealogy.com   **www.genealogy.com/**

Hot tip

If you become seriously interested in genealogy research, you might find it worthwhile to sign up with a commercial service to obtain more detailed information.

Don't forget

Associated websites include Ancestry.com and other country versions such as Ancestry.ca, Ancestry.co.uk and Ancestry.com.au.

Genealogy.com provides three levels of service, depending on the range of data collections you want to access. There's also a free trial so you can make sure that the service is suitable for your needs.

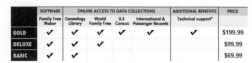

	SOFTWARE	ONLINE ACCESS TO DATA COLLECTIONS				ADDITIONAL BENEFITS	PRICE
	Family Tree Maker	Genealogy Library	World Family Tree	U.S Census	International & Passenger Records	Technical support*	
GOLD	✔	✔	✔	✔	✔	✔	$199.99
DELUXE	✔	✔	✔				$99.99
BASIC	✔	✔					$69.99

8 Spreadsheets

Spreadsheets are a valuable tool, allowing you to manipulate data and perform calculations with speed and efficiency. They include functions to automatically total or average sets of values, and you can create graphs and charts to explore the information. There are pre-defined spreadsheets to help you handle the most frequently required tasks.

Spreadsheets

A spreadsheet is a computerised version of a ledger sheet, an electronic tool for manipulating numbers. It is designed for listing and calculating quantities and values in a wide range of activities, from budgeting and financial analysis, to forecasting and scientific study. The huge advantage of spreadsheets is that once the data is entered, formulas can be created to perform calculations quickly and easily. When any of the component data is changed, the spreadsheet formulas automatically recalculate to reflect the amendment.

Visicalc was the first electronic spreadsheet, followed soon after by Lotus 1-2-3. Microsoft introduced Excel which became its main product for Windows. It provides a wide range of functions including database and query management, pivot tables and what-if scenarios and a full graphing facility.

1   Open Excel to view a standard blank spreadsheet or worksheet. Three worksheets are provided, but more can be added. One or more worksheets comprises a workbook

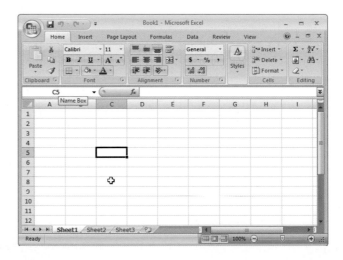

2   Data is entered into cells in columns and rows. Column labels are letters A-XFD, rows are numbered 1-1,048,576

3   A cell is the intersection of a column and row and has a cell or grid reference. The current cell reference, C5, is displayed in the Name Box

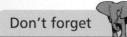

Input Data

1 Both text and numeric data can be entered into a cell. Type your first entry (the worksheet title) and press Enter. The text is stored in the cell and the cursor automatically moves down to the next cell

2 Continue entering your column of data. The text is automatically aligned to the left of the cell

Hot tip

Numbers are aligned automatically to the right of the cell. Initially trailing zeros are dropped, for example 2.25 would display as 2.25 but 5.50 would display as 5.5. See page 142 on formatting numbers.

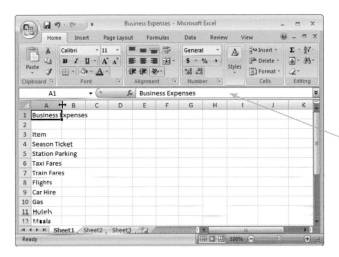

Don't forget

The Name Box and the Formula Bar indicate the current cell and its contents (A1). B1 is empty, although it looks as though it contains some text. If you typed in cell B1, the text in A1 would appear truncated.

139

3 To widen column A to accommodate the length of the text, position the cursor on the header between the A and B to get the double headed arrow. Then drag to fit, or double-click to widen the column to the longest entry

Navigation

- Home key takes you to column A

- End key + directional arrow to the end of the current data range in the direction pressed

- Ctrl+Home goes to A1

- Page up and Page down move a full screen at a time

- Type a name in the Name Box to go to a named range

- Press the F5 function key and type a cell address to Go To

Fill and Copy

To enable swift data entry, Excel provides the Fill tool. It can be used to fill columns or rows with standard entries, such as days of the week or months. It can also be used to replicate standard data, such as regular amounts. For example:

1 Type Sep in cell B3 and then position the cursor on the bottom right hand corner of the cell. When it changes to a large plus

sign, drag across row 3 to fill with months of the year

	A	B	C	D	E
1	Business Expenses				
2					
3	Item	Sep			
4	Season Ticket			Nov	
5	Station Parking				
6	Taxi Fares				

2 Expense items such as season ticket and parking are likely to be a regular sum each month. Complete the entries for September and

	A	B	C	D	E
3	Item	Sep	Oct	Nov	Dec
4	Season Ticket	65			
5	Station Parking	17.5			
6	Taxi Fares				
7	Train Fares				
8	Flights				

then highlight both cells and use the Fill tool to add the figures for the rest of the months

The Fill tool also works with number patterns, as in the examples illustrated here.

  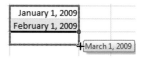

Copy

1 Highlight cell or range of cells and click Copy on the Home tab. Position the cursor where you wish to place the first cell and select Paste

2 The range that was copied will display a flashing outline. Press the Esc key to remove it

Insert, Delete and Move

With your data entered into the spreadsheet, you may find you have omitted a category or misaligned your figures. To insert a column or row:

1 Click on the row or column header and select Insert, Insert Sheet Rows. The row will be inserted above the selected row

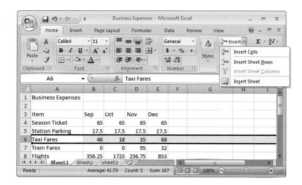

2 For columns the procedure is the same. With columns selected, the program defaults to Insert columns. The new column will be inserted to the left of that selected

3 To delete the contents of a cell or range, just press the Del key. To remove the column or row completely, select it in the header row and click Delete, Delete Sheet Rows

The contents of a cell or range of cells can be moved by selecting them and using Cut and Paste. However, you can also drag them to the new position:

4 With the range highlighted, move the mouse pointer to the edge of the cell where it becomes a four-headed arrow

5 Press the left mouse button to drag. Target cells will be indicated and any contents overwritten

141

Hot tip

The number of columns or rows you highlight is the number that will be inserted into the worksheet.

Beware

Remember that when you insert or delete a column or row, it affects the whole worksheet and may impact items that are not currently displayed.

Don't forget

You can change the contents of a cell by typing new data. Press F2 to edit the contents of a cell without completely retyping. Don't use the spacebar to delete the contents of a cell. This puts a space into the cell which is subsequently treated as text, not as a blank and may cause problems.

Format the Data

Numeric data can be presented in a spreadsheet as percentages, dates or scientific notation. In a new spreadsheet the General, i.e. generic format is used, meaning that text and numbers are displayed as entered. Numbers are aligned to the right of each cell and trailing decimal zeros dropped. To change the number of decimal places displayed:

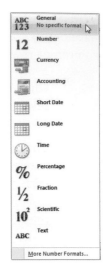

Don't forget

If you choose to display zero decimal places, numbers with decimals will be rounded to the nearest whole number, but only for display purposes. Calculations will include the decimals.

Hot tip

Cells that display a series of ###### simply need widening to display the contents correctly. This often happens if you choose Currency or Accountancy.

1 Select the range of cells to format and on the Home tab, click the Increase or Decrease decimals button

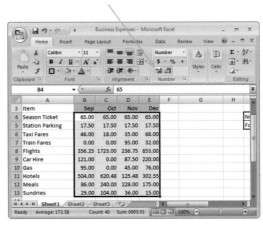

2 Alternatively, for the example illustrated, click the down arrow on General and choose Accounting or Currency

3 Use the Alignment button to align text to the right of the selected cells to match the numeric data and Fill color to highlight headings

4 Excel enables working with dates by allocating all dates a number starting at 01/01/1900. Data entered as 1/12/09, or 1-12-09 will automatically be formatted as a date

Number	1	39459
Formatted as date	1/1/1900	1/12/2008

Autosum

To total a column or row of figures quickly and easily, Excel provides the Autosum function.

1 Position the cursor in the next adjacent cell below the column of figures and click the Autosum button on the Home tab in the Edit section

2 The formula is entered for you with the outlined cells suggested as the range to be totalled

SUM	▼	X ✓ fₓ	=SUM(B4:B13)		
	A	B	C	D	E	F
3	Item	Sep	Oct	Nov	Dec
4	Season Ticket	65.00	65.00	65.00	65.00
5	Station Parking	17.50	17.50	17.50	17.50
6	Taxi Fares	46.00	18.00	35.00	68.00
7	Train Fares	0.00	0.00	95.00	32.00
8	Flights	356.25	1723.00	236.75	853.00
9	Car Hire	121.00	0.00	87.50	220.00
10	Gas	95.00	0.00	45.00	76.00
11	Hotels	504.00	620.48	125.48	302.55
12	Meals	86.00	240.00	228.00	175.00
13	Sundries	29.00	104.00	36.00	15.00
14	Total	=SUM(B4:B13)			
15		SUM(number1, [number2], ...)			

Sheet1 / Sheet2 / Sheet3

3 Click the tick on the Formula bar or press Enter to accept the range

4 The outlined range is merely a logical suggestion. Use the mouse to select an alternative range. In this example, two rows are totalled in one calculation - B4:E5

					Regular
3	Item	Sep	Oct	Nov	Dec	Expenses
4	Season Ticket	65.00	65.00	65.00	65.00	
5	Station Parking	17.50	17.50	17.50	17.50	=SUM(B4:E5)
6	Taxi Fares	46.00	18.00	35.00	68.00	SUM(number1, [number2], ...)

Readily accessible on the Autosum button are other frequently used functions. These work in the same way, for example:

Σ Sum
Average
Count Numbers
Max
Min
More Functions...

1 Position the cursor at the end of the data and click Max to discover your maximum outlay or Average for your average spend

7	Train Fares	0.00	0.00	95.00	32.00	
8	Flights	356.25	1723.00	236.75	853.00	=MAX(B8:E8)
9	Car Hire	121.00	0.00	87.50	220.00	MAX(number1, [number2], ...)
10	Gas	95.00	0.00	45.00	76.00	
11	Hotels	504.00	620.48	125.48	302.55	=AVERAGE(B11:E11)
12	Meals	86.00	240.00	228.00	175.00	AVERAGE(number1, [number2], ...)
13	Sundries	29.00	104.00	36.00	15.00	
14	Total	1319.75	2787.98	971.23	1824.05	

Sheet1 / Sheet2 / Sheet3

Beware

When totaling rows, always check the range Autosum suggests. With figures in cells above it, Autosum will revert to adding columns.

Don't forget

Use the same procedure to calculate spreadsheet rows.

Hot tip

With one column or row totaled, use the Fill tool to copy the formula to the rest of the worksheet.

Beware

Avoid gaps in your data as the outline around the data will stop at a blank row or column.

Calculation

Don't forget

Arithmetic symbols are:

+ Addition
- Subtraction
* Multiplication
/ Division.

Standard rules apply for mathematical precedence, i.e. parentheses ( ) first, multiplication and division, addition and subtraction.

Hot tip

Selecting cells using the mouse avoids typing errors.

Hot tip

Press F4 with the formula created to cycle through the absolute reference options, before you press enter.

As seen on the previous page, the Autosum function allows you to total columns and rows of data with ease, but there are times when a simple formula is required and you have to create it yourself.

1. Click in the cell where you wish to place the calculation and type an equals sign (=). This is a signal to the spreadsheet that this is a formula. Then type, for example, A2*B2 to multiply together the contents of those cells. If the content of either cell changes, the result changes

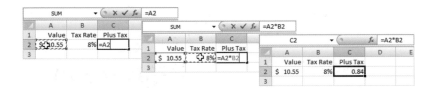

2. Instead of typing, you can use the mouse to select target cells. For example: click in cell C2 and type = then click on A2, type the operator * and click on B2. Then press Enter or click the tick in the Formula bar

3. Cell C2 shows the result of the calculation. The Formula bar shows the contents of the cell i.e. the actual formula

Absolute cell references

Formulas use cell references which are based on the relative position of the cells to the formulas. This means that you can copy formulas from one column or row to the next. To copy a formula based on one particular cell as in the example shown, you need to use an absolute reference. An absolute reference includes the $ sign to fix either the column or the row or both. For example:

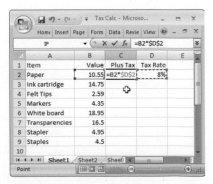

$D2 for absolute column
D$2 for absolute row
D2 for absolute cell

Functions

As well as the very useful Autosum, Excel provides a library of functions to enable a wide range of calculations. To view the list of functions:

1 Click the Formulas tab on the toolbar. The functions are arranged in categories

2 Select for example, Logical and then If. The function arguments window opens with the function syntax broken down into steps

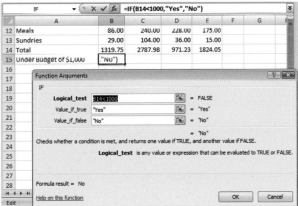

3 Complete the Logical test field by clicking on B14 then typing <1000

4 Add the Value if True (Yes) and the Value if false (No). Then click OK. The completed function syntax is shown in the Formula bar

5 To complete the worksheet, use the Fill tool to copy the function across the rest of the columns

Hot tip

Click the Insert Function button to see the full list of Functions.

Hot tip

If you are unsure of which function you should use, type a description of what you want to do in the Insert Function window.

Don't forget

The example is to discover if our Business Expenses come in under the $1,000 limit.

2787.98	971.23	1824.05
No	Yes	No

145

Auditing Tools

Formula
Auditing ▾

Excel provides auditing tools for you to check the validity of your formulas.

1 Click the Formulas tab to view the auditing options

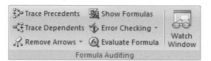

🔀 Trace Precedents	🔢 Show Formulas	
⬜ Trace Dependents	⬥ Error Checking ▾	🔍 Watch Window
🔍 Remove Arrows ▾	ⓐ Evaluate Formula	
	Formula Auditing	

2 Position the cursor on a cell that contains a formula and select Trace Precedents. Select another formula and choose Trace Dependents

	A	B	C	D	E	F
3	Item	Sep	Oct	Nov	Dec	Total
4	Season Ticket	65.00	65.00	65.00	65.00	260.00
5	Station Parking	17.50	17.50	17.50	17.50	70.00
6	Taxi Fares	46.00	18.00	35.00	68.00	167.00
7	Train Fares	0.00	0.00	95.00	32.00	127.00
8	Flights	356.25	1723.00	236.75	853.00	3169.00
9	Car Hire	121.00	0.00	87.50	220.00	428.50
10	Gas	95.00	0.00	45.00	76.00	216.00
11	Hotels	504.00	620.48	125.48	302.55	1552.51
12	Meals	86.00	240.00	228.00	175.00	729.00
13	Sundries	29.00	104.00	36.00	15.00	184.00
14	Total	1319.75	2787.98	971.23	1824.05	6903.01
15						
16	Under Budget of $1,000	No	No	Yes	No	

3 Arrows indicate the data referenced in the formulas

4 Select Show Formulas to have the worksheet display the formula's text, instead of the result of the calculation. Click Show Formulas again to revert to the regular view

	A	B	C	D	E	F
3	Item	Sep	Oct	Nov	Dec	Total
4	Season Ticket	65	65	65	65	=SUM(B4:E4)
5	Station Parking	17.5	17.5	17.5	17.5	=SUM(B5:E5)
6	Taxi Fares	46	18	35	68	=SUM(B6:E6)
7	Train Fares	0	0	95	32	=SUM(B7:E7)
8	Flights	356.25	1723	236.75	853	=SUM(B8:E8)
9	Car Hire	121	0	87.5	220	=SUM(B9:E9)
10	Gas	95	0	45	76	=SUM(B10:E10)
11	Hotels	504	620.48	125.48	302.55	=SUM(B11:E11)
12	Meals	86	240	228	175	=SUM(B12:E12)
13	Sundries	29	104	36	15	=SUM(B13:E13)
14	Total	=SUM(B4:B13)	=SUM(C4:C13)	=SUM(D4:D13)	=SUM(E4:E13)	=SUM(F4:F13)
15						
16	Under Budget of	=IF(B14<1000,"Ye	=IF(C14<1000,"Y	=IF(D14<1000,"Ye	=IF(E14<1000,"Yes","No")	

Manage Your View

When working with worksheets larger than your monitor size, column and row labels disappear from the screen, making it difficult to align data. To keep your data labels in view:

1 Position the cursor below the column headings and to the right of the row headings that you wish to keep in view

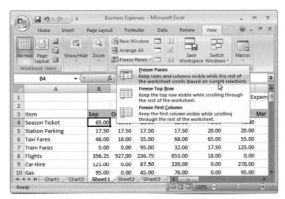

2 Click the View tab, and Freeze Panes. You have the choice of top, side or both

To hide columns or rows within the worksheet:

1 In the heading bar, select the columns or rows you wish to hide

2 Click Format on the Home tab, and in the Visibility section select Hide

Don't forget

Repeat Step 2 to unfreeze frames.

Freeze Panes

147

Hot tip

You can also hide columns and rows by selecting them. Right-click the mouse within the highlighted zone and from the menu select Hide.

Don't forget

To unhide, you must highlight a section that includes the hidden area.

Sort Data

The spreadsheet has a number of database facilities, of which Sort
is a useful example. To sort a range of data:

1 Position the cursor on the cell you wish to use as the
primary sort key and on the Data tab, click the A-Z to
sort ascending, or Z-A for descending. This works with
both alphabetic and numeric data

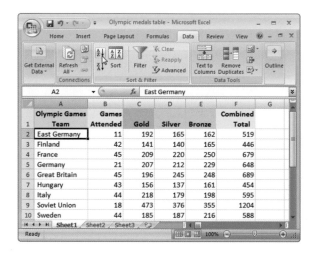

2 Select the Sort button for a greater choice of
options. Click the arrow to choose a primary
field, and a Sort Order

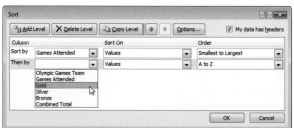

3 Click Add Level to add a second and more sort orders
and then OK when finished

4 Data can also be sorted in date order

Filter Data

The Filter tool, on the Data tab, allows you to select by specific criteria and temporarily screen out unwanted data. For example:

1 With your cursor within the data range, click the Filter button. This adds a series of down arrows to the header line of your data

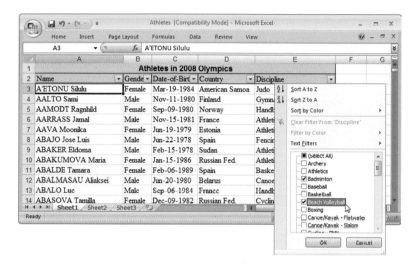

2 Click the arrow on your selected field and choose your criteria, for example one or more sporting activities. Then click OK

3 Choose another criteria, for example Country and repeat the process to extract more specific data

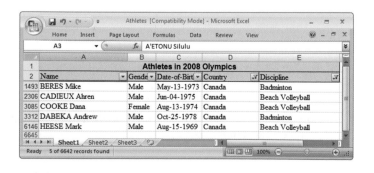

Hot tip

Deselect the Select All box to remove all the check marks. Then select one or more categories.

Hot tip

Use the Text Filters on each drop down menu to add qualifiers such as Equals, or Contains.

Hot tip

You can clear the filter on each column individually or click Clear on the Data tab to remove all filters at the same time.

Print the Worksheet

Hot tip

As spreadsheets rarely fit a standard sheet of Letter or A4 size paper without some adjustment, use Print Preview to save both time and paper. The Page Layout is also available on the View tab.

To view the way your spreadsheet will appear when printed:

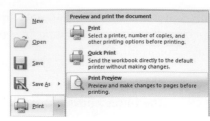

1 Click the Office button, then Print and Print Preview

2 Use Zoom to see how the worksheet fits, and check the number of pages indicated on the Status bar

Don't forget

Once your print layout is selected, dotted lines will appear on the worksheet, indicating the breakpoints for each printed page.

150

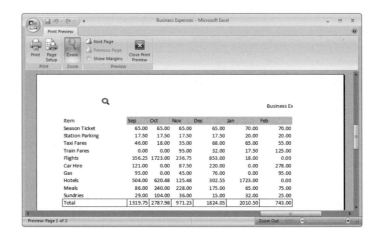

Item	Sep	Oct	Nov	Dec	Jan	Feb
Season Ticket	65.00	65.00	65.00	65.00	70.00	70.00
Station Parking	17.50	17.50	17.50	17.50	20.00	20.00
Taxi Fares	46.00	18.00	35.00	68.00	65.00	55.00
Train Fares	0.00	0.00	95.00	32.00	17.50	125.00
Flights	356.25	1723.00	236.75	853.00	18.00	0.00
Car Hire	121.00	0.00	87.50	220.00	0.00	278.00
Gas	95.00	0.00	45.00	76.00	0.00	95.00
Hotels	504.00	620.48	125.48	302.55	1723.00	0.00
Meals	86.00	240.00	228.00	175.00	65.00	75.00
Sundries	29.00	104.00	36.00	15.00	32.00	25.00
Total	1319.75	2787.98	971.23	1824.05	2010.50	743.00

3 Click the Next Page button to view the rest of the worksheet and help decide on the optimum print layout

4 To change the orientation from Portrait to Landscape, so that the worksheet is displayed more usefully, select Page Setup

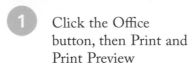

Hot tip

Use the Fit to option to further shrink or enlarge the worksheet to fit to the specified number of pages.

5 Click OK to return to the Print Preview window, from where you can select Print

When the worksheet is printed over several pages, you will need to print the column and row labels on every page.

1 On the Page Layout tab, choose Print Titles. Click in Rows to repeat at top and on the worksheet click to select the row. Repeat for the column

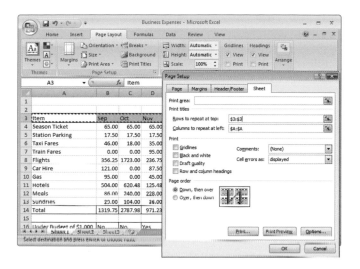

Don't forget

Select a complete range for column or row headings. This would be $A:$A for example.

Hot tip

If you print the worksheet showing formulas, tick the boxes to print Gridlines, and Row and Column headings.

151

To add Headers or Footers to your printed spreadsheet:

1 Click the Header and Footer tab in Page Setup

2 Select for example Custom Footer, and then click in the left section. When you click on File Path, the path and file name of the current file will be inserted

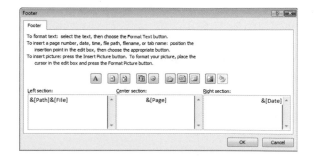

Don't forget

File path and name, date and page number are all examples of autotext. They will be updated automatically.

3 Repeat the action to add page number and date

Charts

Graphs and charts help to illustrate data and highlight trends, patterns and fluctuations.

1 Select the range of data that you wish to chart. This should usually include either a column or row heading

2 On the Insert tab, choose the type of chart you prefer and then select from the options available

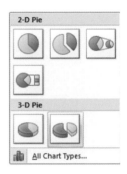

3 The chart will be displayed within the worksheet, complete with a legend and a chart title

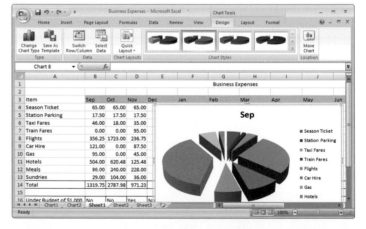

4 Immediately available on the toolbar are coloring options. Click Quick Layout to view different pie chart designs that include adding values and percentages

5 Select the Move Chart Location button to put the chart on its own separate sheet

Whilst the chart is the selected object, the Chart tools tabs of Design, Layout and Format are available. To add details or make amendments to the chart:

1. Select the Layout tab and choose Chart Title

2. Decide on the layout options or choose More Title Options

3. When the chart title frame is added to the chart, click inside it to add the required title text

None
Do not display a chart Title

Centered Overlay Title
Overlay centered Title on chart without resizing chart

Above Chart
Display Title at top of chart area and resize chart

More Title Options...

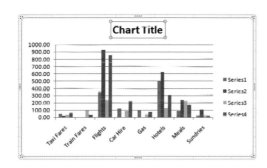

Hot tip

To plot non-consecutive data, select the first range, then hold down the Ctrl key while you click the second or more ranges.

153

The Legend on the right of the chart shows Series 1, Series 2, etc. To correct this and show the actual labels

1. Choose the Design tab and click Select Data

Select Data

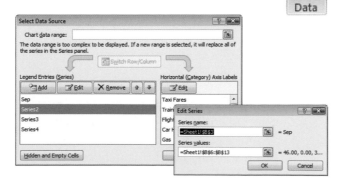

2. Click on Series 1 and then Edit. Choose a label to replace Series 1 and click OK. Repeat for the other Series labels

Templates

There is a large number of pre-formatted spreadsheets included with Excel and many more available on the Microsoft website.

1 Click the Office button and New to view the list

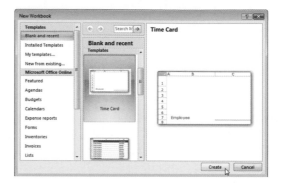

2 Select a template and click Create to open and view the design layout, formatting and predefined formulas

3 When you fill in data on the spreadsheet, you are only affecting the current worksheet, not the original template

4 If you select a template from Microsoft Online, you can choose from Microsoft's own designs or from Microsoft Communities. The templates will be downloaded

Hot tip

Select New from existing to create a copy of a previous spreadsheet. The new file will have the same file name with a sequential number appended.

Don't forget

Any element of the design can be changed to suit your requirements.

Beware

Microsoft does not promise that templates from Microsoft Community will be virus or defect free.

9 Music and Speech

A soundcard can bring your computer to life, allowing you to play music from audio CDs or digital files, listen to radio broadcast over the Internet, and play videos with audio tracks. With a microphone, you can even dictate to your computer.

Soundcard and Speakers

The original personal computer included an internal piezoelectric speaker that was capable of playing one tone at a time. It was really only suitable for warning and error beeps, but with sophisticated programming could play music and sound effects. Fortunately today's computers are equipped with soundcards and speakers that can rival high fidelity audio systems.

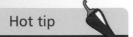
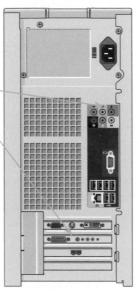

The soundcard will provide connections for various types of speakers ranging from simple stereo speakers to multiple speaker sets with surround sound capability.

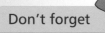

To check the speaker configuration on your computer:

1 Select Start, Control Panel, then Hardware and Sound, then Manage audio devices from the Sound section

2 Select Speakers and then click the Configure button

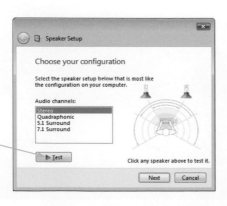

Play Audio CDs

A basic function of your soundcard and speakers is to play an
audio CD (assuming of course you have a DVD/CD drive).

1 Open the CD or DVD drive,
insert an audio CD and then
close the drive

2 The AutoPlay panel is displayed

3 Choose Play audio CD with
Windows Media Player selected

Hot tip

Click in the box Always
do this for audio CDs,
and the selected option
will be carried out
automatically in future,
whenever an audio CD is
identified.

Playing commences but initially the CD is treated as an unknown
album and no details other than the track times are displayed.

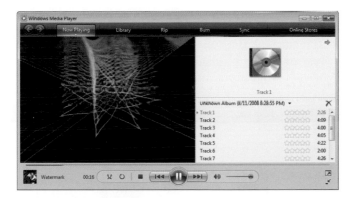

Hot tip

Click Now Playing and
select Visualization to
change the graphic
effects displayed as the
music plays.

If you are connected to the Internet, Windows Media Player will
locate and download information about the CD, and display the
album and track titles and the cover image.

Don't forget

Click the button at the
bottom right, to switch
to compact mode or to
return to full mode.

Media Player Library

1 Click the Library tab to list the music on your system

2 You can sort the contents by artist, album, songs, genre, year or rating, or just display recently added items

3 Press Alt and select Tools, Download, Visualizations to add new effects

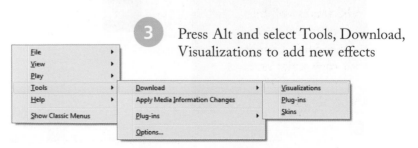

Add Tracks from CD

You can copy songs from an audio CD. This is called Ripping the CD, and Media Player will make file copies that get added to your library. To specify the type of copy:

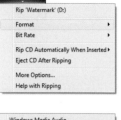

1 Click the arrow at the bottom of the Rip tab and select Format

2 Choose one of the Windows Media Audio (WMA) file formats, or select the MP3 format for greater flexibility

3 Select the bit rate - higher bit rates give better quality but use up more disk space

4 Click the Start Rip button to begin extracting and compressing the tracks

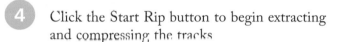

5 The tracks will be stored in your Music folder, with a folder for each artist and a separate subfolder for each album

Beware

Your Media Player may be set to automatically begin ripping when you select the Rip tab, so don't select the tab itself until you have specified the file format and bit rate.

Hot tip

For CDs that haven't been played previously, you'll need an active Internet connection to obtain album details and cover art.

159

Don't forget

You can listen to the CD while you are ripping it (the current track will be left pending until it completes playing) or you can play other content from your library.

Download Music

You don't have to own the CD to add tracks to your Media Player library. Download music from an Online Store.

1 Click the arrow on the Online Stores tab and select Browse all Online Stores

2 Choose a category then select a store from the list provided, for example click Music and then Wal-Mart Music Downloads

3 Click Yes to confirm you want to link with the store

4 Review the suggestions and the collections offered, or enter some search values for an item and click Find

160

5 The search results show the albums and tracks that match

6 Click the speaker symbol 🔊 for an item to play an extract

7 Click Buy MP3 Buy MP3 to download a track or album

8 You will be required to register or log on to complete the purchase and download the associated files

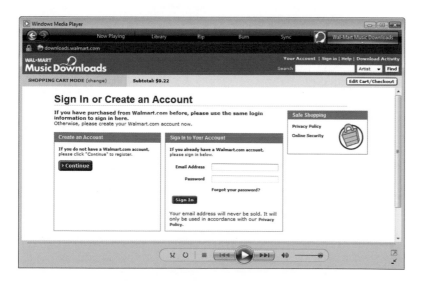

Don't forget

Check that the bit rate offered for the music meets your requirements. In this example, the bit rate is 256kbps.

Hot tip

You may be required to download software to manage the transfer from the online store.

Hot tip

The active online store is shown on the tab. Click the down arrow and select Add current service to menu, to get quick access for future visits.

161

Internet Radio

If you just want to listen to music without saving it on your computer, Media Player can link you to Internet radio stations.

1 Click the arrow on the Online Stores tab and select Media Guide

2 Select the Internet Radio option

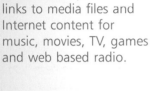

Hot tip

The Media Guide is a website that provides links to media files and Internet content for music, movies, TV, games and web based radio.

Don't forget

You can select a list of radio stations to suit a particular music genre or other content such as news and sport.

Hot tip

The Editor's Picks are displayed, but you can click Show All to see the full list for the selected category.

3 Search by keyword or select a category of radio station, for example New Age music

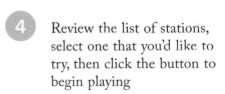

4 Review the list of stations, select one that you'd like to try, then click the button to begin playing

5 Click Yes to link to the radio station via the specified website

6 The selected radio station begins to play

7 Expand the window to see details of the radio station and the variety of channels and other items that it makes available

163

8 Select the back arrow to return to the station selection window, click Recently Played Stations and click a station to expand its details

9 Click Add to My Stations to include it in your shortlist of favorite radio stations

Windows Media Center

If you have the Home Premium or Ultimate edition of Vista, Windows Media Center provides another way to manage your multimedia functions and can turn your computer into a complete home entertainment system.

1. Click Start, then All Programs and select Windows Media Center

2. Choose Custom setup to personalize the configuration

- ○ Express setup
- ● Custom setup
- ○ Run setup later

3. You can optimize your display, set up your speakers or arrange your media libraries

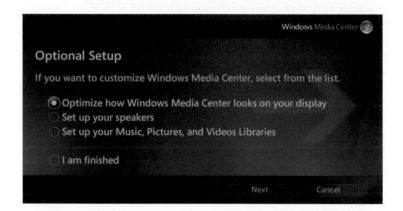

4. The Media Center includes pictures & videos, music, TV & movies, sports, online media and supporting tasks

5 The Music function gives you full access to your music library and allows you to select albums and tracks to play

Don't forget

Like Media Player, Media Center displays the contents of your Music folder, plus any other media folders that you selected during setup.

6 You can watch news, sports and entertainment videos or listen to music and radio via the Online Media option

Hot tip

Select the Settings task to change the way in which Media Center operates. For example, you can choose to always start Media Center when Windows starts up.

7 Media Center provides you with full control of your computer, right through to the Shutdown process

Speech Recognition

One way to interact with your computer is to simply tell it what you want, with Windows Speech Recognition. To set this up:

Don't forget

Speech Recognition is supported in all editions of Vista and is available in the English, German, French, Spanish, Japanese and Chinese languages.

1 Click Start, Control Panel, Ease of Access and then select Speech Recognition Options

2 Choose Set Up Microphone to adjust recording settings

Hot tip

If there are several users of the computer, each user should select Advanced Speech Options, specify a new profile name and complete the setup, then select that profile the next time that user requires speech recognition.

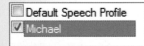

3 Select the type of microphone that you'll be using, a headset microphone being best for speech recognition

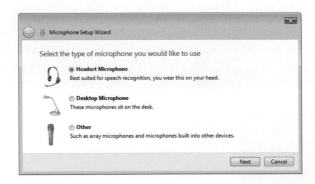

4 Position the microphone as instructed, then read out the text provided, so the microphone volume can be set

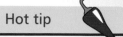 **Hot tip**

If the computer does not pick up your voice, select Start, Control Panel, Hardware and Sound and then Manage Audio Devices in the Sound section, and ensure that the microphone device is enabled.

5 Click Next and Finish and your microphone is set up

6 Choose Take Speech Tutorial from Speech Recognition Options to learn the basic commands and dictation

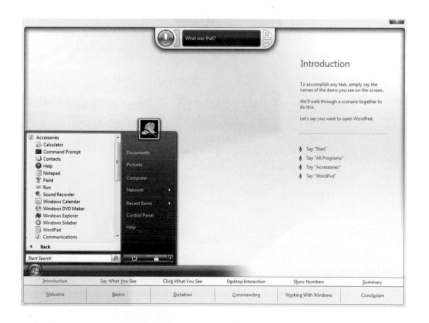

Don't forget

In the tutorial you practise dictation of documents and use voice commands to start and switch between applications and control the system. It improves with use since it adapts to your speaking style and vocabulary, and it provides prompts and questions that help clarify what you mean.

Talking to Your Computer

When you start Windows, Speech Recognition will start up and switch itself into Listening mode.

To see the functions offered:

1 Right-click the Speech Recognition bar

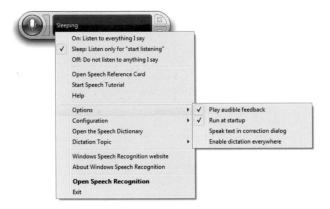

2 Say *Start listening* (or click the button on the bar)

3 Say *What can I say?* to view the Speech Reference Card

4 You can print the reference card. First say *Show all* to expand the topics then say *Print* or click the print icon

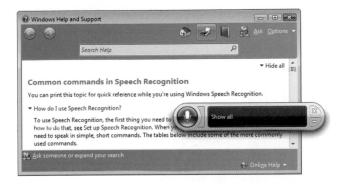

Hot tip

If the computer does not pick up your voice, select Start, Control Panel, Hardware and Sound and then Manage Audio Devices in the Sound section, and ensure that the microphone device is enabled.

5 Open the Speech Recognition Options and select Train your computer to better understand you

Don't forget

You'll get a different set of lines of text each time that you use the training feature, so the computer builds up a complete understanding of the way you speak.

6 Read aloud the text presented a line at a time (it is full of useful tips such as advice to speak out like a broadcaster)

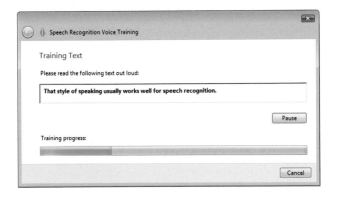

7 When you finish the session you can select More Training if you wish, or just Close

More Training

Text to Speech

You can let the computer talk to you, using the text to speech facilities of the Narrator application.

Narrator

Alternatively, select Start, Control Panel, Ease of Access then Ease of Access Center, and select Start Narrator.

1 Press the Windows Logo key + U to open the Quick Access Center and press Alt+N

From the Ease of Access Center select Use the computer without a display and choose Turn on Narrator, to have the program start automatically when you start Windows.

2 Narrator starts up and you can select the main settings to control what text will be read out

3 Click the Voice Settings button to adjust the voice

There is only one voice currently available, but it does sound very natural. Adjust the speed, volume and pitch to suit your preferences. Narrator will read the contents of the screen, including the text content of programs such as Notepad, WordPad, and Windows Help and Support.

Narrator does not read the text content of programs such as Internet Explorer and Windows Mail, so its value is somewhat limited, in comparison with the more pervasive Speech Recognition.

4 Click the Help command to see a list of keyboard shortcuts such as Insert+F8 (read current document), Insert+F6 (read current paragraph), Ctrl (stop Narrator from reading text)

10 Photography

Optimize the possibilities of digital photography using your computer. It can enable you to organize your photos, add effects, create slide shows and make movies. You can display your digital photographs and videos on your TV through your DVD player, print them or share them with your family and friends on the Internet.

Digital Photography

Digital photography uses electronic technology rather than film, to capture images. These can be displayed, stored, printed, enhanced and shared using computer facilities and software.

When you take a picture with a digital camera, the image is stored on a memory card within the camera. The storage capacity of the card determines how many pictures you can take before you must download them onto your computer or erase them. The higher the capacity of the card, the better, as it means that you can take more pictures before you need to free up space and/or you can capture them at a higher resolution. Memory is extendable, you can buy an extra card, or a larger capacity card.

Resolution is measured in pixels (picture elements). Typically, camera resolution is counted in megapixels or millions of pixels. Most cameras allow you to set a resolution level, but it's best to take pictures at the highest resolution possible, thus getting the clearest image possible. However, the higher the resolution of the picture, the lower the number of images you can store. Also, if you are taking snaps simply for emailing, then choose a lower resolution.

Resolution	Number of pixels
9 million	3456 x 2592
5 million	2560 x 1920
2 million	1600 x 1200
0.3 million	640 x 480

172

When selecting a camera, another consideration is the degree of zoom that the camera can achieve. Cameras have both optical and digital zoom, but the most important is optical. This uses the capabilities of the camera lens to bring the subject closer, enlarging the image before it is stored as pixels.

Digital zoom magnifies the picture by cropping it to select only the specific area after it has saved it as pixels. You can use digital zoom and cropping on your computer using the editing software that comes with the camera or a program such as Windows Photo Gallery. Zooming and cropping on your computer gives you better control over the process.

Other Digital Camera Features

- Antishake mechanism. Digital cameras provide an LCD view finder which necessitates holding the camera away from you when taking a picture. This may cause camera shake and blurring of photos, especially in low light conditions. The antishake feature minimizes or eliminates this problem.

- LCD lightening which increases the power to the LCD screen in sunny conditions when the subject may be hard to determine

- Wide angle lens. This can change the aspect ratio from 4:3 to 3:2 or 16:9 for example

- Scene mode. This feature creates a series of optimum settings for the camera which take into account the usual conditions that prevail at, for example, sunset, in snow, for fireworks etc.

- Video. The more expensive cameras have a limited video function, enabling you to take clips of events

Cameras are packaged with software, a battery pack and charging facility, a USB cable and an AV cable which lets you connect the camera directly to the television.

A Sample Camera

This camera is a Lumix DMC-TZ5 by Panasonic. It has a 28mm wide angle lens and a 10x optical zoom. Its maximum resolution is 9.1 megapixels and it includes features such as Digital Red-Eye and Intelligent Exposure. It is also capable of recording high-definition video at 30 frames per second.

Register the Camera

Register the camera with the manufacturer to receive newsletters and updates to the software and access technical support.

Download or view product documentation, drivers or software by selecting product category and model number below or alternatively enter the model (a minimum of 5 characters is recommended)	

Search

Enter Model Number (if known)	▶ Search
Select a product category	AV Products
Select a product sub category	Digital Still Camera
Select a model	DMCTZ5
Select a document type	Hints and Tips

☐ Show the list in date order. This is advisable for software updates

Don't forget

Some cameras still have a traditional viewfinder which may be an asset if you are unsteady.

Don't forget

Before purchasing a camera, check to ensure that your computer meets the minimum requirements of the camera and software.

Hot tip

Before you install the software, check the manufacturer's site to see if there are any updates.

Install the Software

1 Insert the CD supplied with your camera and select to Run the program

2 Follow the on-screen prompts to allow the program and then select Recommended Installation which will install all four programs

3 The Setup Install shield will step through the process, covering items such as terms and conditions, the destination folder for the files, desktop shortcut, photo acquisition and language

4 Make your choices and the wizard will complete the installation

Transfer the Photos

1 Ensure that the camera is connected to the mains, or alternatively, that it has sufficient power to complete the upload to the PC

2 Connect the camera to the computer using the USB cable or cradle and turn on both the camera and computer

3 The computer should recognize that new hardware is attached and install the drivers for the camera. This will only happen the first time

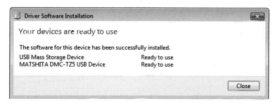

4 The Autoplay window shows that the operating system is treating the camera as removable storage and has allocated it a drive letter. Click the Close button since the camera software will import the pictures

5 PhotofunStudio, the file management and editing program supplied with the camera, offers a preview of the photos and indicates where they will be stored

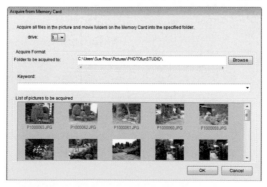

Don't forget

You may have been supplied a card reader with your camera, in which case you will need to extract the memory card from the camera and insert it in the reader.

175

Hot tip

With PhotofunStudio, you can accept the folder suggested, or browse to a different folder. This program will put all the photos into one single folder. Some programs, Windows Photo Gallery for example, will create a folder for each time photos are acquired, usually taking the current date as the folder name.

6 The process is reasonably automated and straightforward

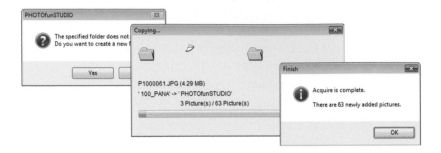

7 When the acquisition is complete, the photos will be displayed, with the Explorer pane showing the folder where the files are stored

Hot tip

The Explorer pane can be used to navigate through the folders. When you select a folder, the images within that folder will be displayed.

8 In common with many other programs that are bundled with cameras, PhotofunStudio has a wide range of tools that will enable you to edit, rotate, add effects and make corrections such as red-eye or crop to eliminate unwanted items in the photo

9 There are also facilities to create desktop wallpaper, send by email, write to CD/DVD and print

Detach the Camera

When the camera is attached to the computer and
switched on, a new icon appears in the Notification area
on the bottom right of the desktop. The camera, with its
memory card, should be treated like any other removable
disk. When you have finished working with it you should use the
Safely Remove Hardware option offered by Windows.

1 Once the photos have been uploaded to the computer,
complete any other action on the memory card, such as
deleting pictures

2 Leave the camera
switched on and
click the icon in the
Notification area

3 Choose the correct drive
to disconnect. When
it is safe to remove
the connection, turn
the camera off and
disconnect the USB cable

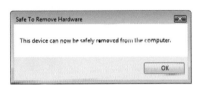

Hot tip

This procedure is
recommended by the
camera manufacturer
and constitutes best
practice. See page 197
for more information
on the Safely Remove
Hardware option and the
problems with incorrect
hardware removal.

Upload additional photos

With new photos added to those already on the memory card:

1 Reconnect the camera as before. This time the software
will recognize that there are additional photos and acquire
only the new images

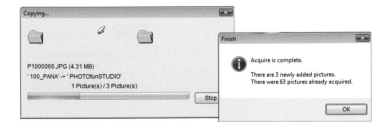

2 In this instance, the files are appended to the same folder,
with other software they may be allocated a new folder

Windows Photo Gallery

You can use the software supplied with the camera to upload the photos to your computer, or there are other ways to transfer them, see page 193. With the images uploaded, Windows Photo Gallery will help you to organize and edit them.

Photo Gallery is supplied with Windows Vista and is fully integrated with the operating system. It is used in this book to illustrate photo file management and some editing and photo manipulation techniques applied to digital photographs.

see page 193.

Hot tip

If you should choose not to install the software provided with the camera, Photo Gallery will start automatically when you select to import pictures and can be used to acquire the images.

1 Open Photo Gallery and it displays Recently Imported photos in thumbnail view

Don't forget

Photographs that were imported with the camera software, rather than Photo Gallery, will not be considered as Recently Imported. You must select Pictures for them to be displayed.

178

2 Photo Gallery recognizes folders where images are stored and includes them in the navigation pane

Hot tip

Click the sideways arrow to expand the folder list and the down arrow to contract it.

3 To add a folder to the list, click File, Add folder to Gallery. You can select folders on other drives and even across a network

4 To view all the pictures in the listed folders, click All Pictures and Videos, or just Pictures

Descriptive Tags

With all these photographs now resident on your computer, how are you going to manage to arrange them into logical groupings? The answer is to add tags. These can be selected by Photo Gallery to identify and display matching photos. To see how tags work:

1 Click Tags in the navigation pane. The sample images provided with Vista illustrate various tags

179

Hot tip

Click a star to rate those photographs that are especially good.

2 To create your own tags, click Create a New Tag. Type the name and it will be added alphabetically to the tag list

Don't forget

Photographs are date stamped by the camera. They can be selected by date in Photo Gallery, so make sure that you keep the correct date in the camera.

3 Now choose the photographs that you wish to tag. Hold down the Ctrl key as you click to select individual images, or the Shift key to select a block of consecutive images

4 Use Add Tags in the Preview pane to select the tag to use. When you click the tag in the navigation pane, the chosen photos will be displayed

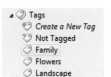

Edit Your Photos

Lighten or Adjust Contrast

1 Select the image and click Fix on the toolbar

2 Click Adjust Exposure and slide the pointers either way until a satisfactory result is achieved

3 You can undo individual changes or revert to the original settings. When you click Back to Gallery, any changes made will be saved

4 If at some point in the future you should wish to retrieve the original picture, repeat the steps and this time choose Revert. Windows retains details of the original image

Adjust Red-Eye

Red-eye can still be a problem in certain conditions, even though cameras now have the built-in double flash to try to eliminate it.

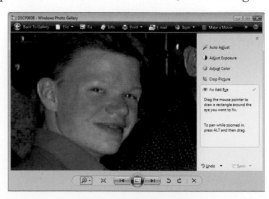

1 Choose Fix, Fix Red Eye and draw around the problem area to recolor

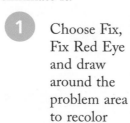

Crop the Image

1 To remove unwanted elements, click Fix and Crop. Use the four-headed arrow to move the frame to outline the required area

on't forget

Cropping the image is using digital zoom to magnify an area.

2 If the frame size should need adjusting, choose from the pre-defined aspect ratios. Then click Apply

Don't forget

The aspect ratio you should choose for your photo depends on how you wish to view it.

If printing choose 4 x 6, TV or PC choose 4 x 3, widescreen or HD TV use 16 x 9.

Add Captions

With Photo Gallery, adding a caption adds a title to the photo. The title is only visible when the photo is selected either in Photo Gallery, or in folder view.

Hot tip

If you intend to print the photograph yourself, you can choose the Custom aspect ratio to stretch or shrink the frame.

To add visible text, such as greetings or place name, you would need to use a more sophisticated editor.

Print Your Photos

The most cost effective way to view your photographs is to write them to a CD or DVD and view them, either on your computer, on a TV or on a DVD player. (See page 187). There are times, however, when you will want to have them printed. There are four main approaches:

- A dedicated photo printer. These usually print 4 x 6, but some are available to print 5 x 7 or a variety of sizes. You may have to buy the photo paper from the printer manufacturer. Most of these printers can be used with the memory card from the camera, or directly from the camera with Pictbridge software

- Take the memory card or a CD of the photographs to a local printing service. Many are now semi-automated with the customer running the process

- Upload the photographs to an online photography site, where you can invite friends and family to view the pictures, and have them printed. This is generally the cheapest method

- Print them using your regular color printer. This is best suited to when you want the convenience of an instant print, or if you wish to print a non-standard size

Photo printing in Windows Vista

1. Open Photo Gallery and select the pictures you want to print. Press Ctrl+A to select all the photos, or Ctrl and click for individual pictures

2. Click the Print button and Print

3 The default is to print one picture per page. Scroll down to view the variety of layouts offered

Don't forget

Note that with four to a page the print size is 3.5 ins x 5 ins, not the standard 4 ins x 6 ins as in commercial printing.

4 With four pictures to print, selecting a different layout will reduce the print to one page

5 Choose a print quality. The benefits of higher resolution printing are marginal as the printer has to interpolate the extra pixels and printing will be slower

6 Paper quality has the greatest impact on the resulting print. However, remember that some printers cannot handle high gloss finishes. Click Print when ready

Order Prints

If you choose the option to order prints, Vista will access the Internet to locate online photography dealers suitable for your location. Companies that you investigate will be added to the menu. See page 190 for an alternative way to order prints online.

Hot tip

When you click Send Pictures, you will be warned that personal details might be sent to the chosen printing site. You will be able to get an idea of cost etc. before you start entering personal details.

183

Integrated Facilities

Slide Show

Hot tip

Right-click the first slide
and select Preview to
step through the slides
with the adjustment
tools, and rotate and
delete accessible.

1 Choose a folder in Photo Gallery and click the Slide
Show button at the bottom of the window

Don't forget

Slideshow is also
accessible in folder view
for folders that contain
recognized picture
formats such as .jpeg,
.bmp, .tiff etc.

2 The slides will display full screen, with a time delay of
approximately seven seconds. Speed up the show by
clicking on the screen to move to the next slide. Press Esc
on the keyboard to end the show

Email
Take advantage of the link provided to access Windows Mail and
easily adjust image sizes as they are attached.

1 With one or more
images selected, click
the E-mail button

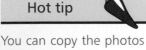

Hot tip

You can copy the photos
to a CD or DVD as a
data disk, to share with
family or for security,
using the Burn facility.

2 Choose a resolution,
remembering that the
larger the file size, the
longer it will take to
send and receive. This
is especially important on a
dial-up system

3 Complete the recipient's
address field and your
message in the usual way.
Then click on Send

Video Clips

Video clips have a different file format from a standard photo, and there are several formats used including .avi, .mov, .mpeg and .wmv. To play a video clip from your camera, you will need a player that supports the specific file format. The Panasonic camera produces a .mov video clip which runs in Quicktime, but can also be handled by Realplayer. The .mov format is not recognized by Photo Gallery, but is able to run in the enhanced Windows Live Photo Gallery. To set this program as your default viewer:

1 Open the program, click on File, Options, select the Import tab and click Change Default Autoplay options

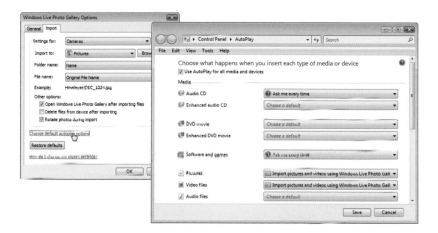

2 On Pictures and Video files choose to Import using Windows Live Photo Gallery. Then click Save

3 Import the video clip as you would a photograph. Clips are displayed as both a single photograph and with a film-style border

4 Double-click on a clip to run the video

Movie Maker

Hot tip

Windows Live Movie Maker is due to be released as part of the Windows Live family of software.

Don't forget

You can import directly from your video camera into Movie Maker. Click File, Import from Digital Video Camera.

Hot tip

To help organize a large number of files in the Collections pane, create folders to separate them into logical groups. Click File, New Folder. Then click on the New Folder name and rename it appropriately. Images and other media can then be dragged and dropped into the folders.

Windows Movie Maker can be used to give a professional appearance to your photos, videos and video clips by adding transitions and effects, music and voice-over, titles and credits. When finished, you can save the movie to DVD and play it on TV, email it or share it on the web.

1 Open Windows Movie Maker and click to Import Media. Browse to select the photographs or media you wish to use in your movie

2 To select all the photos, click the first and press shift and click the last. To select individual photos, hold down the Ctrl key as you select. Then press Import

3 The imported items will be placed in the Collections pane from where they can be selected and placed onto the storyboard

4 Click the Automovie option to see a movie created and run by Movie Maker. This will give a suggestion of some of the effects that can be achieved

5 Click Undo to clear the storyboard for you to create your own movie

Make Your Own Movie

1 Drag the pictures to the storyboard in the required order. Photos will initially be added to the end of the movie strip, but can be inserted or moved when necessary

Hot tip

Picture duration is set to 5 seconds. Click Tools, Options and the Advanced Tab to alter it.

2 In Storyboard view, click Transitions. Drag the selected transition to the space to the left of the photo

 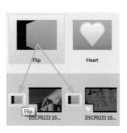

Don't forget

Transitions affect the way one slide changes to the next slide, for example fading or revealing from left to right. Effects are displayed on the slide itself, for example panning across or zooming in.

3 Switch from Transitions to Effects. Add Effects to the corner of each photo and run the Preview to see how the slides are displayed

4 Click Storyboard and change to Timeline to enable further adjustments

...cont'd

Don't forget

Right-click any photo to change or remove the effect.

5 Use the Timeline zoom buttons to enlarge your view of each image so that you are able to extend the display time of individual photos

6 Click the Show Tasks button and in the Edit section, choose Titles and Credits

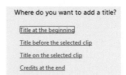

Hot tip

When you hover the mouse over an audio track, it shows the length of the track. Use this to help you select a track suitable for the length of your show.

7 When you add the Title, you have the option to change the title animation and also the text font and color. Add Credits to roll up the screen at the end of the show, as in professional movies

8 Import audio or music to add your movie. Then drag and drop it on the Audio/Music line. This can be adjusted to the movie length by stretching or shrinking to fit

Hot tip

Click Tools, Narrate Timeline to add your own commentary to the movie.

9 Right-click the Audio/Music bar to access options such as Fade in and Fade out

10 Click File, Save Project to save your movie. The Project will be saved into the Videos folder. These are relatively small files as all they are saving are pointers to the various media that you have incorporated into your show

Publish Your Movie

1 With Movie Maker and your chosen project open, click Publish Movie

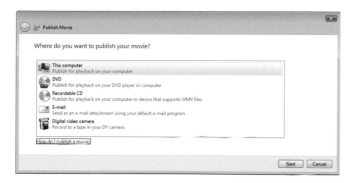

Don't forget

To choose DVD as your media, you need a DVD writer and a copy of Windows DVD Maker. This is included in Windows Vista Ultimate and Windows Vista Home Premium.

2 If you select DVD, Windows will save and close your project and open DVD Maker with your project listed. To include more projects click the Add items button

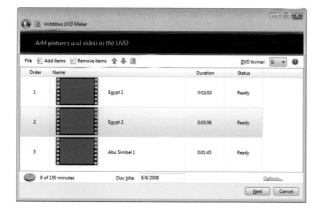

Don't forget

With DVD Maker, you write the whole DVD in one session. Make sure you assemble enough clips to make good use of the disc. Other DVD writing software may provide the option to append clips.

3 Use the up and down arrows to change the playing sequence and add a title for the disc. Click Next

4 Add Menu Styles to create an opening screen for the video. At this point, you can also customize the menu and add menu text. Click Preview to see the video play and make any final adjustments. Then click Burn to copy the movie to the disc

Share Photos on the Internet

1 Choose an Internet site that offers free photo sharing such as **www.kodakgallery.com**

2 Register your name and email address and click the option to Share photos

3 Click the Upload photos button. Kodak will create a new album for you with the current date. Provide a name for the album and click Continue

Share photos.

Upload your photos in a snap - your family and friends can enjoy them with just one click.

● Share photos

Hot tip

Kodak, in common with other online photography sites, has software that can be downloaded to enable more efficient selection of photos.

4 Browse to select the pictures and then click Upload. The upload may take several minutes

5 Click the option to Share Album. You will be prompted for the recipients' email addresses and a Subject

Don't forget

On the Kodak site there is no restriction on who can view the photos. Although you may only invite a few people to share, recipients can pass on the invitation. Some sites will request a password to restrict viewing to invited guests.

6 Tick the box to Require friends to sign in. When they view your photos, their name will be added to your Guestbook and any comments they make

7 Click Send Invitation when the required fields are completed. The recipients will get an email inviting them to view the album

11 Gadgets and Gizmos

Computer electronics on a smaller scale are applied to create storage devices for many purposes, ranging from digital photographs, videos, maps, driving instructions, or just simple extension of the storage on your computer. Software functions within Windows or specially installed for specific devices enhance the function of these devices.

Extra Storage

To see how much disk storage you have on your computer:

1 Select Start and click Computer (or press WinKey+E)

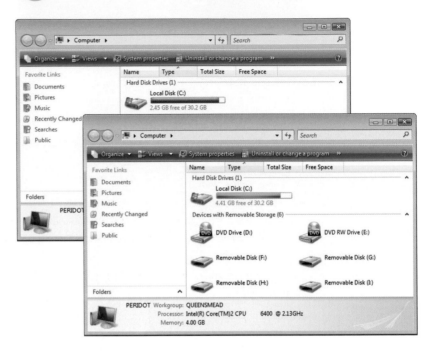

2 Look particularly for Removable disk entries which could indicate that you have a media card reader installed

If your computer has a media card reader installed, you'll be able to extend your storage space using memory cards. These come in a variety of shapes and sizes and will typically provide 1GB to 8GB or more additional file space, depending on type.

Each GB of storage on the memory card can store around 300 music tracks, about 350 high definition photos (depending on resolution), about 30 minutes video clips or any data files to fit.

Reading a Memory Card

1 Insert for example a Smart Media memory card

2 Choose the option to Open folder to view files

3 The contents of the memory card will be displayed

Hot tip

The exact contents of the panel displayed when you insert a memory card depend on the type of files contained. This shows the response when there are picture files on the card.

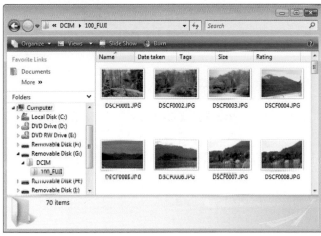

Don't forget

This is an alternative way to access and copy the photos on your digital camera's memory cards, rather than the supplied software (see page 174).

4 To remove the memory card, click Computer to display the Drive view, select the relevant drive (in this case G:)

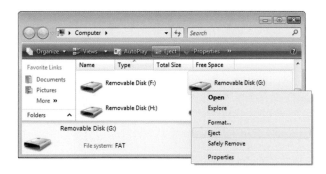

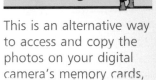

Hot tip

With a multiple drive media card reader, you do not use the Safely Remove option (see page 197) since this would disconnect the whole reader until the next restart.

5 Click the Eject button (or right-click the drive and select Eject from the menu displayed)

Flash Drive

Memory cards are fairly delicate. For storage that you can carry around with you, try the more robust USB flash drives that offer anywhere from 64MB to 32GB, in a compact, durable and high speed format. Most USB flash drives have a removable cover over the USB connector. However, some are designed with a sliding mechanism so the connector is hidden until needed.

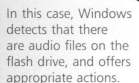

Hot tip

In this case, Windows detects that there are audio files on the flash drive, and offers appropriate actions.

1 Insert the flash drive into one of your USB ports

2 Windows assigns the next available drive letter and displays the AutoPlay list

3 Select the option required e.g. Open folder to view files

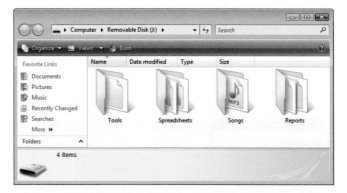

Hot tip

Close any folder views or programs using the flash drive, before choosing to safely remove the device.

4 Click the Safely Remove Hardware icon and select the drive, then click OK when the confirmation appears

External Disk Drive

For larger volumes of data, you can add an external disk drive. This device includes a drive similar to the internal hard disk in your computer, but fitted into a separate disk enclosure. Some such devices use the standard 3.5 ins disk format found in desktop computers. Others use the 2.5 ins drive found in laptop machines, to reduce the power requirements and avoid the need for a separate power supply unit.

1 Plug in the power adapter if required then connect the drive to one of the USB ports

2 If required, Windows installs the device driver software

3 Click the message bubble to view the software details then click Close to continue

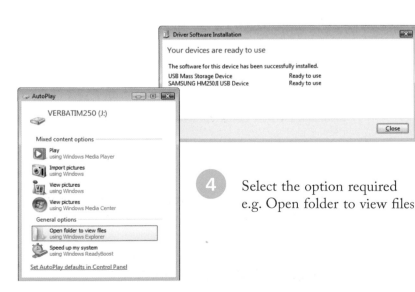

4 Select the option required e.g. Open folder to view files

...cont'd

When the device is attached, Windows assigns the next available drive letter, as with flash drives.

Don't forget

The device is recognized as a hard disk and positioned in that section of the Computer folder, alongside the C: drive.

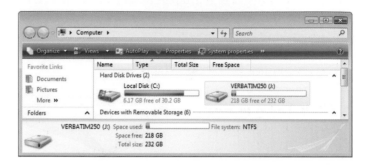

If you select Open folder to view files, or if you double-click the drive icon in the Computer folder, the root level is displayed

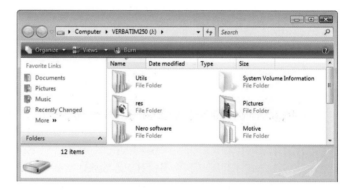

 Click Safely Remove Hardware and select the drive, then click OK when the confirmation message appears

Beware

Do not remove the drive immediately, but close any windows or applications referencing that drive then try again later. If the problem persists, it may be best to shut down before removing the drive.

 You may be warned that the drive is currently busy

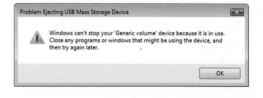

Device Removal

You need to take care when removing drives because Windows may be in the process of updating the contents. To see the options, view the drive properties:

1 From the Welcome Center, double-click View Computer Details and select Device Manager

2 Click the [+] to expand the list of disk drives

3 Right-click a drive (in this case the internal hard drive) and select Properties

4 Click the Policies tab

For internal drives, Windows sets Optimize for Performance, and offers to enable write caching on the disk. There are two levels, but the advanced level requires some form of power backup on your PC.

5 From Device Manager, right-click a USB connected drive

6 View the Policies for the removable drive

For USB drives, Optimize for Quick Removal is the default setting. You can select Optimize for Performance, but this isn't recommended due to the potential risk to your data.

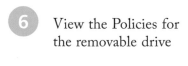

TomTom GPS

Don't forget

Other devices include storage facilities, for example digital cameras (see page 172), personal digital assistants (PDA) or global positioning systems (GPS).

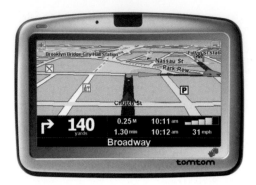

The TomTom GPS is an example of a device that functions on a stand-alone basis but connects to your computer for updates, backup and data transfer. This will require computer applications, in addition to device driver software as used by the flash drives.

Hot tip

You can install the software from the CD provided with the device, but you'll get the most up to date version if you visit the TomTom website.

The TomTom GPS uses the Home Dock to connect to your computer via one of the USB ports. It also requires the Home device management application to be installed on your computer.

1 Go to the website **www.tomtom.com/home,** and scroll to the TomTom Home download links

Don't forget

For illustration we use TomTom GO920 and the Windows version of the Home application.

2 Click the link for your GPS type and operating system version and follow the prompts to Save the software to disk

3 When the download completes, click Run to install the software

4 Select the Installer language and the Setup Wizard begins

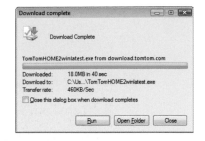

5 The Wizard will install the Home application

6 Install completes and Home will be started up

7 Click Log In to sign on to the TomTom website, using your email address and password

199

Connect the GPS

Don't forget

While the device is connected to your computer, the battery will be recharged. For a quicker recharge, leave the device switched off.

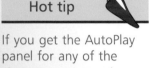

Hot tip

If you get the AutoPlay panel for any of the storage components on the GPS, just click the Close button. The Home application will be started automatically.

Hot tip

You can store digital pictures and audio tracks on the memory card and play them through the GPS speaker (or over the car radio).

1 While signed on to the TomTom website, connect the GPS using the Home dock and a USB port

2 Switch on the GPS and press YES to make the connection with the computer

3 The first time you connect, Windows identifies the device and installs the drivers required

4 Choose to work with the Internal Memory or with the Memory Card (if fitted)

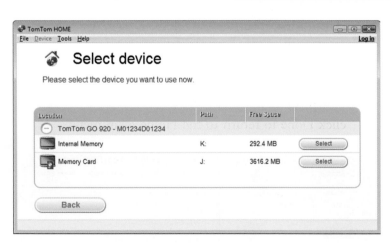

5 The Home application will connect to the TomTom server and search for updates for your particular device

6 Home searches for updates and downloads them onto the hard disk on your computer

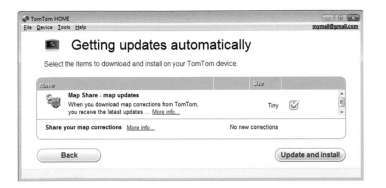

Don't forget

If TomTom Home does not automatically start the check for updates, click Update My Device in the main menu.

7 Select the updates that you want and click Update and Install to apply changes to your device

Hot tip

You may be offered a number of updates but you do not have to apply them all at once. Just click to clear the tick symbol against updates you want to postpone.

201

8 When the changes have been transferred and applied, click Done to return to the Home main menu

Beware

Do not disconnect the device while the update is in progress or you may corrupt the contents.

Back Up Your GPS

1 From the main menu select Backup and Restore

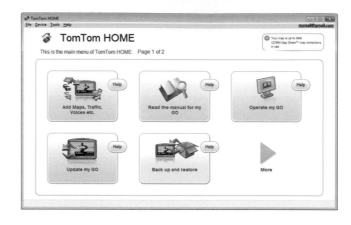

2 Click "Back up now" to begin copying the contents of your GPS onto the hard disk

3 Around 4GB of data will be copied to the disk

4 When backup completes, click Done to display the menu

5 Click the More arrow to see the other functions offered

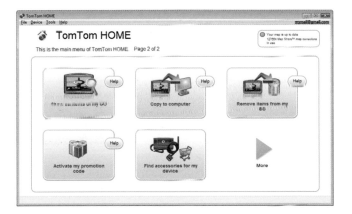

Don't forget

Click Show Contents to list all the facilities stored on your device. To save space, copy infrequently used items to your computer then remove them from the device.

6 When you finish working with your GPS, click Tools, Disconnect Device

Hot tip

You can disconnect and switch off but leave the device plugged in to complete the battery recharge.

7 You can now safely remove your GPS with all its memory

Media Players

These connect to your computer so you can transfer the MP3, JPEG, AVI or other media files that they handle.

The devices may use computer software such as Windows Media Player or device specific applications, to sync and transfer media files, or the devices may simply appear as removable drives to which you can copy files.

For normal operation they are stand-alone devices. For storage they use memory cards (up to 32GB) or hard drives (up to 160GB). They may rely on headphones or external speakers and there may be no display. The Sony Walkman MP3 player for example connects to your computer just like a USB flash drive, but stores MP3 or WMA audio files that you can listen to via a set of lightweight headphones.

Media Players handling digital photos usually feature a display, ranging in size from 1.8 ins to 7 ins. They may support multiple types of memory cards, and are often used to complement a digital camera, allowing you to view the photographs more effectively when you are without access to a computer or television. They may also include a built in speaker, useful for replaying audio tracks or video clips with sound.

Windows Vista treats devices such as these as removable drives, so you must:

1. Attach the device to your computer and Windows will load the associated software driver and application

2. Amend or supplement the contents of the device adding appropriate media files from your hard drive

3. Use the Safely Remove Hardware feature when finished with the device, to avoid the risk of losing data

Don't forget

Another type of storage device is the digital player, which handles MP3, JPEG, AVI or other media files to play audio tracks or display digital photos and videos.

Hot tip

These devices can be quite sophisticated. Sony's Sports Walkman NW-S200 for example includes a pedometer and has a Music Pacer feature that plays music based on your speed, giving you fast or slow music depending on your jogging performance.

Personal Data Assistant

The Personal Data Assistant or PDA is a fully independent device, with its own operating system, for example Windows Mobile. It will have its own set of applications, which could include Microsoft Office Mobile, with mobile versions of Outlook, Word, Excel and Powerpoint. PDAs such as the HP iPAQ Business Navigator go further, adding 3G mobile phone capability and GPS navigation. Some models also include a 3 megapixel camera.

Before connecting your PDA to your computer you need to install the appropriate software.

1 Insert the CD provided with your PDA, select the language and choose the Setup and installation

2 Follow the prompts to install the programs required to connect and synchronize your PDA

Don't forget

The PDA is another stand-alone device with its own storage that connects to your computer to share functions and data.

Hot tip

The installation program detects which operating system you are running and offers Microsoft ActiveSync for Windows XP or earlier, and Windows Mobile Device Center (WMDC) for Windows Vista.

Hot tip

The installation CD also includes product manuals in PDF format, links for additional tools and information on accessories.

Set Up and Sync Your PDA

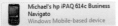

1. Windows detects a new device, installs the device drivers needed and configures the software

2. When the setup completes, the WMDC software is launched and the connection made

3. Click Set up your device

4. Specify the types of information you wish to synchronize

5 Windows will compare the contents of the PDA and your computer and synchronize them with the latest contents

Hot tip

There are sync settings to control how much data is synchronized. For example, the default setting for Calendar is for all future appointments plus the past two weeks.

6 You'll see for example the contents of your calendar from Outlook 2007 copied to your Outlook Mobile calendar

Don't forget

While connected, you can browse the contents of your PDA from your Windows system.

7 Similarly, if you have chosen to synchronize files and folders, any new or updated files will be transferred

Hot tip

To terminate any file activity towards the PDA, click the Sync Center icon in the System Tray and select Stop All.

8 Switch off the PDA when you want to disconnect

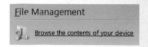

207

Home Network

Don't forget

The devices we've looked at so far are connected to the computer as secondary devices, even if they have independent capability, so they didn't form a true network. Now we'll try connecting computers to each other.

If you have more than one computer, you can share their storage facilities and other devices. To do this you need to connect them together as a network. This map shows a typical home network:

Wired Computer   Router / Switch   Internet

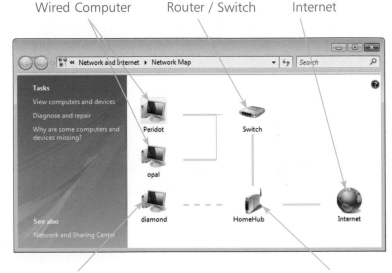

:   Wireless Computer   Wireless Access Point / Gateway

The computers are connected via ethernet cables to the network switch, or via a radio link to the wireless access point. The router connects the network to the Internet and this connection can be shared by any of the computers on the network. To add a PC and create or extend a network:

Hot tip

Many computers have an ethernet network adapter. If not, you can fit an internal adapter to a desktop PC, or add a USB or PC Card adapter to a laptop PC.

1 Add a network adapter card (if not already fitted) and restart the computer

2 The icon in the notification area tells you that there is initially no network

3 Connect the Peridot computer to the network router switch using an ethernet cable

4 Click Start, Network to show the networks available

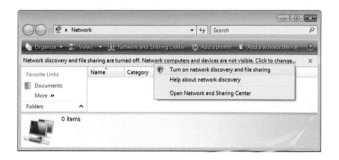

Hot tip

Windows Vista will automatically recognize and connect to the network if Network Discovery is turned on.

5 If Network Discovery and File Sharing are turned off, click the message and select Turn On

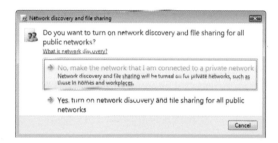

Beware

Do not turn on Network Discovery for public networks (such as those at airports, hotels or Internet cafes).

6 Select Private Network discovery then view the contents of the Network and Sharing Center

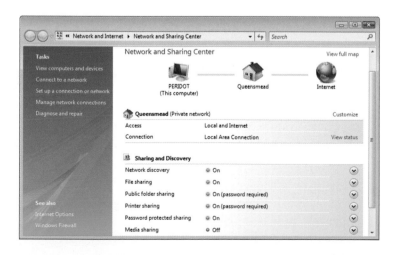

Don't forget

Although files and printers will be set for sharing, Password Protection ensures that they can only be accessed by people with a user account and password on the computer.

Share a Drive or Folder

When you have networked a computer, you can share its facilities with other computers on the same network. For example, to share access to the hard drive on the Peridot computer:

1 Open the Computer folder, right-click the C: drive and select Share

2 Click the Advanced Sharing button, click in the box to Share this Folder, then click OK and close the Properties

3 The drive is flagged with an overlay on the icon to show that it is now being shared over the network

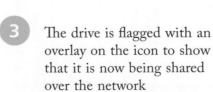

You can now share the resources of the Peridot computer.

1 Click Start, Network on another networked machine, in this case the Diamond computer

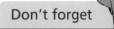
2 Locate Peridot in the network list and double-click the computer icon

3 You'll be prompted to sign in with a user name and password valid for that PC

4 Click OK to connect

5 You can now access the items available for sharing, in this case the C: drive, plus the Public folder and the printers

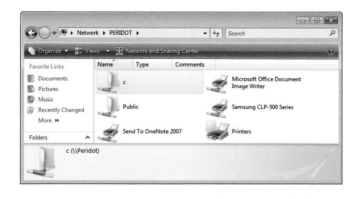

Wireless Network

If your router has wireless capability you will be able to connect computers with wireless adapters, without using network cables.

1 Click the network icon and select Wireless Networks are Available

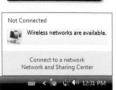

2 Select the wireless network desired

3 Click the Connect button

4 Enter the key code and click Connect

5 The computer is linked to the network and the Internet and in future it will be automatically connected

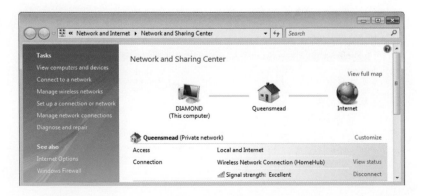

12 Manage Your Computer

To keep your computer and Windows operating system working effectively, you need to maintain the system and update the software on a regular basis. Fortunately, Windows provides all of the tools that are required to carry out these tasks.

Windows Update

Don't forget

You can also double-click View computer details from the Welcome Center, or right-click the Computer entry in the Start menu and select Properties, to display the System Properties.

Windows Vista operating system needs regular updates to ensure that it remains safe and efficient. To see the level of your copy:

1 Click Start, Control Panel, System and Maintenance, System

2 If it shows just the Windows edition, you have the original release without updates

3 The newer release will be described as Service Pack 1 (SP1). This includes many of the updates available

4 To check the status of your system, click Windows Update to see if automatic updating has been enabled

Hot tip

If Automatic Updating for Windows is turned on for your system, you will already have received SP1 and all the subsequent updates and be fully up to date.

5 Click Turn On Now for Automatic Updating and Windows will check for available updates

Don't forget

You can click Change Settings to make adjustments to the way Windows Update operates, for example to change the time that updates are applied.

6 Click Install Updates to download and install the updates

Hot tip

The first update may be major, since it will apply all the outstanding updates, so it is best to complete it at a time when your computer is not busy.

7 Your system may need to restart to complete the updates

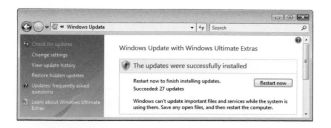

Beware

Windows will configure the updates during shutdown and upon restart. Make sure that the computer is not powered off during these processes.

Ultimate Extras

If you have the Ultimate edition of Windows Vista, you'll find that there are some optional updates that you can download.

1 Click the link to View Available Updates or the link to View Available Extras to see the list of optional updates

2 Select the items required then click the Install button to download and install the applications

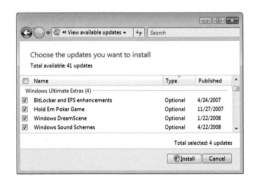

3 After installation, you may be offered further extensions

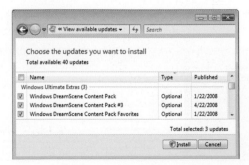

4 When you've installed all the components, make sure that you have Windows Aero active on your system (see page 37)

5 Select Personalize, Desktop Background and set Location Windows DreamScene Content

(see page 37)

Don't forget

The DreamScene feature requires Windows Aero support to be active on your system.

Hot tip

You can fit the video to the display, or you can choose to keep the aspect ratio of the original video.

217

6 Select a video and click OK to make it the background

Beware

DreamScene takes a considerable amount of processing power. When running on a laptop that is battery powered, the video will be replaced by a still image.

Microsoft Update

1 Select Start, All Programs, Windows Update and select the option to Get updates for more products

2 At the Microsoft Update website accept the terms of use and click the Install button

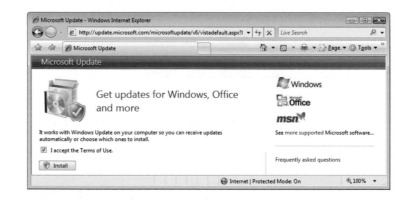

3 Select Windows Update to display the combined service

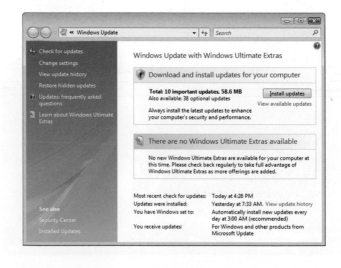

Security Center

1 Select Start, Control Panel and click the option Check this computer's security status

Security
Check for updates
Check this computer's security status
Allow a program through Windows Firewall

Don't forget

You can also open the Security Center by selecting the link on the Windows Update window.

See also
Security Center
Installed Updates

2 Click Find a Program to locate an Antivirus program

Hot tip

This website shows a variety of security products suitable for Windows Vista. The suppliers usually offer trial versions of their products and sometimes include a free version for personal use.

3 Install for example AVG Antivirus (see page 31) and the warning indicator will be removed from the Security Center

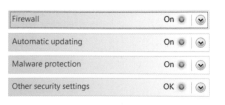

Manage Devices

Windows can help you locate and install the device driver software required for components on your system. For example:

1 Windows may indicate that a particular device such as your soundcard is unavailable or unsupported

2 Open System Properties (see page 214), and click Device Manager then review the warning or error indicators

3 The ! symbol on a device entry indicates that the device concerned is in a problem state and requires attention

4 Double-click that device entry to review the device status

5 In this case, the drivers are not installed so click Reinstall Driver

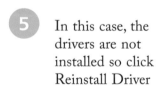
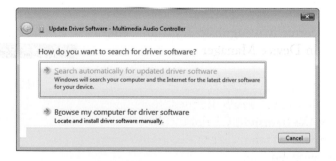

6 Click Search Automatically to have Windows search on your computer and on the Internet for a suitable driver

...cont'd

7 Windows will install the driver if found, or inform you if it was unable to find a driver

Don't forget

You can also open the Security Center by selecting the link on the Windows Update window.

8 If required, visit the website for the manufacturer (in this case www.creative.com) and locate a driver for download

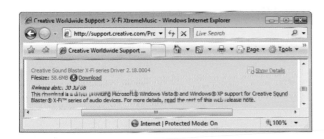

Beware

If your computer supplier provided a customized OEM version of an adapter card, you may have to go to that supplier's website to find the appropriate driver.

9 Run the downloaded file to install the driver and then restart the system if required

10 You should see that the device is now correctly recognized and fully defined in Device Manager

Repeat this process for any other devices that are not fully defined, for example the Samsung CLP500 color laser printer for which Vista does not have a driver built in.

Hot tip

The Device Manager will now show the device in its correct location with the appropriate description.

221

Maintain Your System

Don't forget

As well as keeping your software up to date, you need to keep your hardware in trim, the hard drive in particular.

Hot tip

You can choose which categories of file to delete, and view a list of the specific files if required.

Beware

You may have to press F5 to update the details displayed for the drive in the Computer folder.

1 Open the Computer folder. If the hard disk shows up colored red, you know it's too full

2 Right-click the drive icon and select Properties

3 To free disk space, click the Disk Cleanup button

4 Choose to clean up files for your user name or for all users on the computer

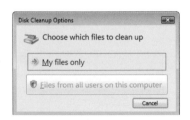

5 Confirm which files to delete and click OK

6 Disk Cleanup calculates how much space you may be able to free up

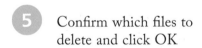

7 Confirm file deletion and the available space on the drive is increased accordingly

If you are experiencing problems with your hard drive, you can tell
Windows to search for and correct errors.

1 Open the Properties for
the drive and select the
Tools tab

2 Click the Check Now
button then click Start

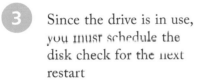

3 Since the drive is in use,
you must schedule the
disk check for the next
restart

```
Checking file system on C:
The type of the file system is NTFS.

A disk check has been scheduled.
To skip disk checking, press any key within 5 second(s).
```

4 On restart, the disk check will start up automatically

```
Checking file system on C:
The type of the file system is NTFS.

A disk check has been scheduled.
Windows will now check the disk.

CHKDSK is verifying files (stage 1 of 3)...
  68288 file records processed.
File verification completed.
  73 large file records processed.
  0 bad file records processed.
  2 EA records processed.
  44 reparse records processed.
CHKDSK is verifying indexes (stage 2 of 3)...
31 percent complete. (28511 of 91152 index entries processed)
```

5 Windows will be restarted when the disk check completes

Defragment Your Drive

Each time the system makes changes to files on your hard disk, the new data may be stored at a different location. Over a period, the contents of the disk become fragmented. This may slow down the system while it reads from different places to load the parts of the files required. You may be able to improve the performance of your system by defragmenting your hard disk.

Beware

When you select Defragment Now, the process may take minutes or hours, but there's no progress bar, so you'll just have to leave the system until it completes.

1 From the Tools tab in hard disk properties (see page 223) click Defragment Now

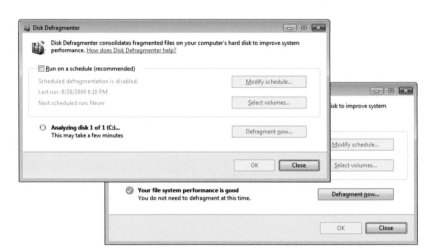

2 Your disk is assessed and you'll be told whether or not you need to defragment at this time

If you Defragment on a regular basis, the disk will remain well ordered and the task can be allowed to run in the background.

3 Click in the box to defragment on a scheduled basis. The default is Wednesdays at 1:00 AM (or next restart) but you can select Modify Schedule to change the details

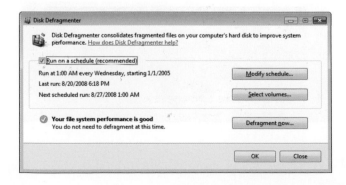

Hot tip

System Restore

By default, Windows Vista creates a restore point every day, and also just before any significant change such as installing a program or a device or applying a system update.

If things keep going wrong with your system after a change, you can restore it to its previous state and get it working again.

1 Click Start, type part of **system restore** and click that entry when it appears at the top of the Start menu

2 Select Recommended Restore, or click Choose a different restore point if you want to go further back

3 Choose the appropriate restore point and click Next to confirm and restart the system with the earlier settings

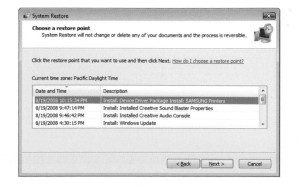

Restart in Safe Mode

1 Click Start, click the arrow next to the Lock button and select the Restart option

2 Press F8 repeatedly as the computer restarts (after the initial computer logo but before the Windows logo)

3 The Advanced Boot Options menu will be displayed. Select Safe Mode with or without networking, as you require and press the Enter key

Hot tip

Safe Mode will start up Windows with a limited set of files and device drivers, without all the usual startup programs and services. This checks that the basic settings function correctly.

Beware

Sometimes Windows will detect a problem with the last session and start up automatically in Safe Mode. Shutdown and restart the system and Windows will usually clear the problem and restart in normal mode.

Don't forget

You can use tools such as System Restore (see page 225) to make corrections from within safe mode. Restart Windows and allow it to complete normally to end Safe Mode.

If you find it difficult to display the Advanced Boot Menu, there's an alternative way to restart in Safe Mode.

1 Click Start, type **msconfig** and press Enter

Don't forget

When you enable Safe Mode via the Msconfig Safe Boot option, Windows will restart in Safe Mode until you select a different option.

2 Click the Boot tab, click Safe boot and choose Minimal, then click OK and click Restart to start up in Safe Mode

3 When you've finished working in Safe Mode, run **msconfig** again, clear the Safe Boot box, and choose Normal Startup from the General tab

227

4 To check out the startup items, run **msconfig** and choose the Selective Startup option

Hot tip

If you suspect one of the Startup items, click Disable All, then Restart and add the items back one at a time, restarting after each addition. In this way, you should be able to determine which item is causing problems.

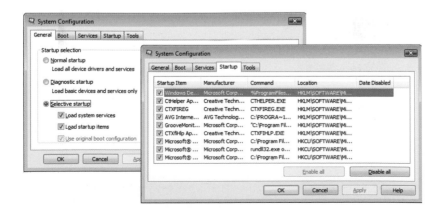

Backup and Restore

To keep your system safe, Windows can help you back up files to a hard disk, to a removable disk or to writeable CDs and DVDs. To run the backup process:

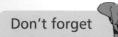

1 Type **backup** in the Start Search box and select Backup and Restore Center

2 Choose Back up files to schedule regular copies of data files such as pictures, music and documents

3 Choose Back up computer, to make a complete copy of the entire contents of your computer

4 When you have problems with files on your system, you can choose Restore files to recover data files and folders, or Restore computer to recover the entire disk

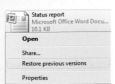

Glossary

A

Adapter Card – card which plugs into a slot on the motherboard, to add facilities and interfaces for attaching peripheral devices

ADSL – a very fast data transfer method that uses normal phone lines to handle phone calls and data transfer at the same time. Download rates of 512 Kbps up to 8 Mbps

Antivirus Program – a program which finds and eliminates computer viruses

Application – a computer program that provides a particular set of system or business related functions

B

Backup – a copy of a file or set of files

Bay – place in a computer case to put drives and other devices

BIOS – Basic Input/Output System. A limited set of instructions to the computer which gets it started

Bit – short for "binary digit", a single on/off position in a digital number, and the minimum unit of data

Booting – Starting up the computer and initiating the operating system

Buffer – location for temporary data storage while processing is going on

Button – a graphic which when clicked upon executes a command or function

Byte – 8 bits of data, usually a single character

C

Capacity (Disk) – amount of data that can be stored, measured in megabytes or gigabytes

CD-R – recordable compact disk on which, with the appropriate type of drive you can copy data files, in a one time write only operation

CD-RW – re-writable CD disk, on which, with the appropriate type of drive you can save data, erase and write fresh data

Cell – intersection of row and column in a table or on a spreadsheet

Chart – a graphical representation of data

Clip Art – pre-drawn pictures to add to documents

Clipboard – a section of computer memory used to temporarily hold data that has been cut or copied for transfer to another document or location within a document

Columns – columns of data side by side, as in a newspaper

Commands – special codes or keywords that tell the computer to perform a task

Copy – duplicate selection onto Clipboard

Cursor – symbol marking where text will appear when you type

Cut – remove selection from document and store temporarily on the Clipboard (an area of computer memory)

Data Recovery – program which tries to recover deleted or damaged data

Data Compression – method used to store data in less space

Database – a program to manage and manipulate lists such as addresses, phone lists and inventories

Debug – look for and remove errors in a program

Default – the original settings; what will happen if you don't change anything

Defragment – puts files on storage disk so that the whole file is in sequence rather than scattered across the disk

Delete – remove selected object (not saved anywhere)

Desktop Publishing (DTP) – program which gives precise control of where and how text and graphics appear on the page

Directory – a grouping of files, more usually known as a folder

Disk Management – program involving formatting and defragmenting your disk

Download – transfer a file to your computer from elsewhere on a network or the Internet

DPI – dots per inch. Used to measure printer resolution

Draft Quality – quality good enough for a test print or for internal use

Driver – file that gives directions to the computer on how to use a device connected to the computer

Edit – make changes in a document

Email – electronic mail - sending messages over a network or internet connection

Executable File – a file which runs a program, also known as an EXE file

External Device – plugs into a port on the computer or connects via wireless communications

Field – a single item that is part of a record in a database

File – something saved on the computer - a document or program

File Transfer – moving a file from one computer to another

File Management – program to help you create, move, rename, delete files

File Name – has two parts: Filename and Extension, in the form filename.ext

File Type – file name extension which identifies the type of file, for example doc, txt, htm or exe

Folder – a grouping of files

Font – typeface for character set, and associated with Size and Style

Footer – text at the bottom of a page, that is repeated throughout the document

Footprint – amount of physical desk or floor area that a device requires

Format (Disk) – makes the disk ready for use and removes all existing data

Format (Document) – arranges the appearance of the document by selecting the typeface, font size, spacing of lines and words, etc

Formula – an equation used to calculate values for interest or mortgage payments

Freeware – program which is given away for free

FTP – File Transfer Protocol. A protocol for moving files between computers

Full Path Name – lists the route to a file starting with the drive name and naming all the folders/directories, like c:\documents\memos\Report4.doc

Gateway – connects networks of different kinds

Graphics – pictures and charts

Hard Copy – Document or file printed on paper

Hard Disk – large capacity data storage device, usually non-removable

Hardware – the physical parts of the computer

Header – area at the top of a page that is repeated on every page of the document

Icon – a small graphic which when clicked runs a program, executes a command or opens a document

Input – everything you tell the computer

Input Device – device used to give the computer data or commands. Includes keyboard, mouse, scanner, etc

Insert – add text at location without overwriting existing text

Internal Device – plugs into a slot inside a computer

Instant Messaging – a program which notifies you when your contacts are online. You can write them messages which they receive instantly

Justification – alignment of text: left, center, right, full

Keyboard – input device with keys for letters of the alphabet, numbers, and various symbols

Kilobyte – 1024 bytes historically, though often used to represent one thousand (1000) bytes

LAN – Local Area Network. Computers connected together in a single location

Layout – arrangement of text and graphics

Liquid Crystal Display (LCD) – screen type used in laptops and for flat panel monitors

Liteware – a free version of a program which is missing some high-end or desirable features

Logon – procedure where user must identify himself to the computer to continue

Macro – small program to automate actions within a major application

Main Memory – where the computer stores the data and commands that are currently being used, also know as RAM (random access memory)

Margin – space at the borders of the page or other document object

Megabyte (MB) – 1024 kilobytes historically. For data storage devices and telecommunications a megabyte is one million (1,000,000) bytes

Megahertz (Mhz) – 1 million cycles per second

Memory Management – program to handle where RAM programs put their data

Menu – a list of available commands which may contain other commands as a submenu

Modem – device which translates between the analog phone line and the digital computer. From Modulate/Demodulate

Motherboard – main circuit board of the computer

Nag Screen – screen message that reminds you to pay up each time you run a shareware program

Nanosecond (Ns) – 1 billionth of a second. Used to measure memory speed

Nesting – putting directories or folders inside other directories or folders

Network – a set of computers which are linked together on a permanent basis

Newsgroup – a discussion group on the Internet where messages and responses are posted for all to read

Node – each device connected to a network

OCR Software – software which changes a scanned document from an image to editable text

Operating System – the instructions that the computer uses to tell itself how it works

Orientation – direction the printed page runs: portrait or landscape

Output – data that has been processed into useful form

Partition – a portion of a hard disk. Disks have separate partitions for different operating systems or to store data separately

Paste – place clipboard contents at cursor location

Pixel – one dot on a screen, comes from picture element

PPM – pages per minute. Measures printer speed

Print Preview – displays how the document will print as opposed to how it looks on the screen

Query – a way to arrange records in a particular kind of order or to show only the records that match certain criteria

Queue – the set of print jobs waiting to be done

RAM – main memory (random access memory), which is volatile memory that is erased when power is turned off

ROM – read only memory which cannot be changed. Contains the instructions to start the computer

Refresh Rate – how often the picture is redrawn on a monitor

Removable Media – storage media that are removed from the computer, such as flash drives, CDs and DVDs

Router – connects networks and controls the traffic of data among the networks

Scanner – device that captures a whole page and converts it to digital image

Server – a computer which handles network tasks and data

Shareware – software which you may try for a limited time before purchasing

Shut Down – close all programs and turn off computer

Soft Copy – displayed on screen or by other non-permanent means

Spacing – space between letters or lines of text

Spell Checker – program which looks for spelling errors

Spreadsheet – program for handling numeric data, like budgets, financial statements and sales records

SQL – structured query language for commands that create database queries

Table – a set of rows and columns

Touchscreen – monitor screen that reacts to being touched by finger

Tower – Vertical case for a personal computer

Trojan – short for Trojan horse, a program that allows others to access your data, to record your logins and passwords, or to destroy or alter data

Typeface – a set of characters of similar design

Undo – reverses whatever change you just made

Upgrade – to replace a program with a newer version of one you already have

Upload – transfer a file from your computer to another

USB – Universal Serial Bus, a connection that can be used by a wide range of devices, rather than each device having a unique connector

User Profile – a set of preferences for a particular user.

Utility – a program that performs tasks related to the maintaining of your computer's health - hardware or data

Vector – a means of defining an image in terms of geometric shapes. Used by drawing programs

Virus – a computer program that performs tasks without your consent. May be harmless but annoying or may be highly damaging.

Window – a rectangular area of the screen which displays a program's user interface, a document, or a system message

Wizard – an automatic set of steps that lead you through a process

Word Wrap – automatically wrapping the text to the next line so it all fits within the page

Worm – An unwanted program that duplicates itself across a network. It uses up storage space and resources and can interfere with the ability of the system to function

Write Protect – method that keeps data from being over-written

WYSIWYG – what you see is what you get, displaying results on the monitor as they will appear when printed

Index